SEA LIKE A MIRROR

– reflections of a merchantman –

ALAN JONES

Whittles Publishing

Published by
Whittles Publishing,
Dunbeath Mains Cottages,
Dunbeath,
Caithness KW6 6EY,
Scotland, UK
www.whittlespublishing.com

© 2005 Alan Jones

ISBN 1-904445-16-0

*All rights reserved.
No part of this publication may be reproduced,
stored in a retrieval system, or transmitted,
in any form or by any means, electronic,
mechanical, recording or otherwise
without prior permission of the publishers.*

Typeset by
Sharon McTeir, Creative Publishing Services

Printed in the UK by
Bell & Bain Ltd., Glasgow

Contents

Preface		v
Chapter 1	A SHIP LIKE NO OTHER	1
Chapter 2	THE NEW BOY	6
Chapter 3	FRANKIE	14
Chapter 4	TOMMY AGAIN	25
Chapter 5	IT WAS MY WATCH	37
Chapter 6	NO ONE BOTHERED WITH NAMES	49
Chapter 7	A JOLLY GAY CAPTAIN	58
Chapter 8	A SLIGHT DISRUPTION	69
Chapter 9	THE SHIP IS YOUR HOME	80
Chapter 10	AMERICAN DREAM	93
Chapter 11	LOSS OF DOSS	107
Chapter 12	FILIPINO MONKEE	125
Chapter 13	A SORT OF ASSASSIN	152
Chapter 14	THE WORST SEA DAY	163

Preface

When called upon to report the weather, the sailor has a book of coded messages where he may record by number the sea's state, the cloud cover, and the force of the wind. The calmest of seas – that having the appearance of glass, whose oily surface is ruffled by nothing more than a flying fish's wings, is given a zero and ascribed the description 'Sea like a mirror'.

This happy condition has an effect far removed from writing weather reports and is enough to spellbind a well-seasoned mariner having little better to do with his time than lean upon his taffrail and gaze down into the depths. Reflections such as these generate an inspiration to write and after a life of seafaring can be so arranged as to form a book. This is such a volume.

Now, in the era of satellite navigation and container ships, it should perhaps be regarded as a recent history. My *aide mémoire* in this regard has been my dear wife, Judy Gray, who though mostly absent when it all happened, can remember from my letters and stories better than I. It is probably not appreciated that wives of seafarers have a harder life than their more inflexible husbands. Affections that were bestowed upon children are instantly transferred to the home-coming sailor, while he may critically review her management of the homestead in his absence! I dedicate this book to all these ladies, a brave and formidable race indeed.

My grateful thanks are also due to: Mary Godwin at the Cable and Wireless Museum at Porthcurno; Diana Parker at the Port of Seattle Main Office; Richard Alexander MIPR, Consultant Archivist & Historian for the Furness Withy Group; and C.P. Alers, Secretary at the Stichting National Sleepvart Museum, at Maassluis. All provided photographs or snippets of information, which are very much appreciated.

Alan Jones,
North Devon

Chapter One

A SHIP LIKE NO OTHER

―

The smell from the river flats filled the streets, making its mark on my memory. For some distance along the bank, small houses of honey coloured Kentish brick rose up on either side, guiding me through the township of Greenhithe, the whole of which was dusted grey from the cement rendering plant at Swanscombe. I had missed my connection at Charing Cross, and, now late, hurried through the village with quickening footsteps. It was all so alien to the new boy from Gloucestershire. Then, by Crouch's boat yard, the broad brown river showed. Almost salt, the Thames in her lower reaches wore forever her perfumes of brackish water drying in pools, and weed on the tidewashed mud.

The ship, which resembled a hulk, sat so high in freeboard that she seemed ready to topple, a monstrous thing, striped black and white. This was the Thames Nautical Training College, H.M.S. *Worcester*. Lying a couple of cables offshore she was immovably tied at each end by anchors screwed deep into the mud. She was closed for the end of term with her duty boats bobbing idly at their buoys.

Ingress Abbey, an administrative building in the grounds, was the place set aside for interviews, a procedure having the air of conscription about it. The Selection Committee occupied their chairs about a directors' table, like jackdaws round a chimney pot. We were inside the big room at the abbey.

'Jones apologises for being late,' said the secretary, 'he missed his connection.'

The Board, seeming more mindful of student subscriptions, deprecated with small shrugs, 'Now. Why do you want to go to sea?' they said, kindly.

It was almost a formality. The stage, so soon, seemed set. I was in! But did I really want it? On the train I had developed misgivings. It had all started with a fifteen year old, too eager by half to escape grammar school, and full of silly conceits about how well a naval officer's uniform would hang upon his frame. There was none of the visceral yearning for the sea. Nor any knowledge of it, but for a hazy mind picture with the ugly bits airbrushed out, of a colourful *Treasure Island* and pages such as the 'River Amazon as far as Manaos' from my school atlas. Two years membership of the Sea Cadet Corps had put down an errant seed, and *Worcester* was seen, by my seniors, as a satisfactory conclusion to undistinguished scholarship.

There was no going back now. Their acceptance letter was eclipsed by the outfitting list, bestirring my mother to sweep me down to Silvers, the Eastcheap tailors, for three pairs of this and that, an expensive Burberry, a uniform of shiny black doeskin with gilt buttons and a regulation cap as flat and round as an old seventy-eight rpm record.

The hat, I later found, served as a sign of status. On that dismal day of joining, we found the older boys had distorted the tops by removing the whalebone and buckling them into a more raffish style around shapes of coathanger wire. But this privilege, I discovered, was confined to fourth termers and above. On that day, new boys wandered miserably from deck to deck in a daze. Homesickness, a most deadly ailment, had set in quickly and we sought the company of others the same, whom we recognised by the unused hang and newness of their clothes. The only escape, for which we fretted through those first interminable days, was the oblivion of sleep. This came, but not before we had mastered our hammocks – a controlled straddling like mounting a horse – and a number of boys had tipped out and onto their sea chests. Sleep, the briefest sojourn, and then, upon the order, the run, the unquiet run up ladder upon ladder, to the head and the short harassed minute for morning ablutions.

Not only were hats a sign of hierarchical power. New boys were subject, at will, to scrub a senior's lanyard or even to warm up a toilet seat in the icy cubicles which lined the forecastle's washrooms. There was violent punishment for transgressors without leave of appeal. For not doubling across the games room (a law unknown to me) that area's cadet captain pulled me up, told me to touch my toes and laid across my rear with a broomstick breaking it into three pieces. Protests were useless, as day to day authority lay in the hands of retired naval C.P.O.s only a few generations removed from the cat o' nine tails. The ultimate power lay with the Captain Superintendent, a distinguished VC from the earlier war, whose governing ability was now, unhappily, on the wane.

Six months or so after settling in I found myself crewing this gentleman's gig, a white craft of some beauty maintained for his private use. The boat, with a single bank of oars, was equipped with royal blue thwart pads, a polished brass yoke, and canvas covered pudding fenders. The order to take the captain ashore consisted of a specific warble on the bosun's pipe (each different bidding had its own warble) followed by the boy-bosun's summons, issued very loud,

'Awaaay first gig !', and whether we were eating, at study, or relaxing on the lower decks we must jump up and hurtle down to the boat platform. We took pride in our rowing, practising up and down Long Reach in the dawn light until our bottoms bled, and in races beat all challengers who frequently turned up from naval vessels and the like. Oar propelled boats were a necessity as all people and supplies were ferried from a wooden causeway accessing the foreshore. The working tier boat brought bread and milk – and schoolteachers – at the break of day; heavy double banked cutters or 'barges' carried larger groups of boys to sports events, or route marches when the ground was frozen, and clinker built whalers, long and sleek, were used for the races.

Races and swiftness were not a feature of the schoolrooms tucked down in the stern end of the lower deck, with their academic subjects cruelly emasculated to make way for Seamanship. No national standard was followed, and our 'passing out' document took the form of a yellow parchment awarding an ordinary, first class, or first class extra certificate. These official pieces of paper had no curriculum with which to measure them and so, happily, escaped criticism. But there were prize days – great happenings with taut white awnings reaching over decks scrubbed to a whiteness in the July warmth and the paddle steamer *Royal Eagle* disgorging our fazed parents at the gangway. We lined up for our prizes, before joining them and taking passage back up to the Tower Pier and blissful release for the holidays.

Seamanship was crammed into us from the beginning. First principles saw us sitting on our sea chests with short lengths of tarred rope, worn limp by generations of boys, learning from our naval instructors to knot and splice, serve, whip and parcel. In the classrooms an officer worked through the dog-eared tome which remained our seamanship bible for years. Rhumb line navigation and traverse sailing were dispensed by a retired convoy commodore, together with the mysteries of the spherical triangle in celestial position fixing.

We were led by the nose into the world of ships and the elements of the sea. It was not in our blood, yet, but it had a way of intruding itself.

Worcester was, in that last term, presented with a set of steel masts and yards, relics of a dismantled old reserve hulk. It was not boys' work. Contractors and a floating crane with lifting gear shipped the masts, (but not before we had dutifully placed our good luck pennies under the mainmast heel) and swayed up the yards. This addition,

*The **Worcester** at Greenhithe*

plus a little wishful imagination, bestowed on her the august appearance of a seventy-four of Nelson's time, as each mast had its top – and topgallant sections. The high new masts were an open invitation to the reckless, to scale them before the shrouds (stays out to the ship's side) had been set up. This did happen one night and by the greatest bad fortune the Captain was first to see his new wonders defaced. Someone had climbed to the maintop and deposited an article of coloured clothing, which flew out flaglike, ugly and impudent. Word came down. Lots of very strong words.

The accountability for the upper deck and its masts, and, by association, removal of offending pennants, lay with the First Class Cadet Captain of the Fore Division, who happened to be me.

'Come on, Jones,' my small clique of friends had cried, on the day the mast was shipped, 'you know you don't mean it. Who wants to fall and break his head open, *you*?'

'No. Of course I mean it,' I replied, as they guffawed, 'I'll climb that mast, yes, even as it is, with shrouds still not set up.'

It was not an act of showy courage, heights had fascinated me, since, as a boy, I climbed the tall pear tree at the bottom of my garden. The offending garment was retrieved before the day grew much longer. The fifty-foot ascent, hand over hand over loose hanging shrouds had offered a delightfully shivering challenge. I would show then that I could match the midshipmen of Nelson's day, who made a word out of 'skylarking.' This incident has stayed in my memory as showing up a metaphorical 'Jolly Jack' within me. There would be a good many confrontations with this oddity in the years to come. The awkward fellow managed to reflect my ambition, while remaining unhampered by my scrupulosity.

Aloft or alow, during that last term, our looks were daily outward at the river, with our thoughts on a future employer. Soon we would choose the shipping company that had most appeal. This frangible selection was reached by uninformed conjecture and a shallow judgement of their ships, a choice left entirely to us. I have never been able to understand why no better guidance was given, from those above us, for this ultimate selection would influence dramatically the course of our lives.

The long river reaches presented a daily parade of beautiful ships from every company making their way to and from the Royal Docks, and, on a clear day the mists would lift enabling us to see Tilbury, and the funnels of the great passenger ships which lay there. The company with the most garishly coloured or racy ships with raked bows would be the one to find favour, as though we picked cars for the track at Silverstone. This resulted in some regrettable choices. All the ordinary fellows joined the big passenger companies which 'Jolly Jack' found slavish and predictable. The gaudiest funnel went to Australia, and he wouldn't want the lack of glamour in that. In this way Furness Withy's Prince Line, with trading world wide and a varied fleet of ships attracted my preference. Interviews were arranged.

Chapter Two

THE NEW BOY

We were recalled to Furness House soon after interview for the final nod, which would come, we knew, from Mr. Bottomley. This time we made do with the rear entrance. An unimportant niche door in Fenchurch Street opened onto a stone staircase just wide enough for two. This access could not compare with the high glass portals through which we had stumbled on our first visit. Artless and awed, we had crept through the main revolving doors in Leadenhall Street. We crossed the main hall, bigger than a cathedral and lined with marble. Ranks of typists hunched over their machines tapping echoes into the ceilings. We found the lady in 'Personnel' holed up in the basement. She appeared not to notice us, but after a chilly pause had said, 'You should use the rear entrance, everybody else in the Company does.'

It wasn't much better this time. She threw a look at the spare waiting chairs and a flicker at us. 'Just sit there,' she said, 'he won't be long.'

The Manager of Sea Personnel was forty minutes late back from lunch. The poise with which he carried his bulging waistcoat and high wing collar made it plain that he had every right to be late back from lunch. And that two cadets, not yet seventeen, with three years to go before they had any value at all as Second Mates, could well afford to wait. He settled a black stringed pince-nez, eased into a desk, and started to speak. Tired homilies came wrapped in homely Essex accents but a crunch came at the end. He reminded us of the mothers who had borne us, hence the sanctity of all womanhood.

'Remember now, you boys, just stay out of the bars and that sort of place in ports abroad. And keep away from the women you meet in 'em. We don't want you coming home with more than you left, now, do we?'

'No sir.' An embarassed response, not fully comprehending.

He got up, and with the puffy exertion came the suggestion of lunchtime whisky.

'We are sending you both to the *Pacific Enterprise*. She is refitting in Manchester Drydock, sailing in a week or thereabouts. Now. If the first thing you see when you go on board is a loose rope's end – I've told so many lads – don't just pull on it. Find out firstly where it goes.'

But even Bossy Bottomley could never know what lay behind the high brick wall which edged the Trafford Road. Excitement and apprehension were pushed to their limits, as, even from the top deck of a Corporation bus, the wall blocked off any first sightings of the ships, their cradling drydocks, or anything else. We tripped over her, it seemed, before sighting her, for the hull of *Pacific Enterprise* lay hidden in the depths of her graving dock, and her decks were awash with welders' cables and acetylene bottles resembling a factory wasteland. All that marked her out as a ship was the tall Furness funnel standing up like a beacon, and for which we aimed, plodding through puddles dyed black by factory swarf. The company livery lay fresh upon it, laid on by loyal hands in time for her arrival home, in fat and thin bands of damson and black. The bow and stern were submerged below the dock wall sills, but her name was still visible on the convoy boards that hung each side of the navigating bridge.

Mr Pocock, the Mate, was inspecting the newly cement-washed fore-peak tank. Told to pull on our boiler suits, we followed him down into the cavernous darkness on our first early lesson in Ship Construction.

World trade since the war had boomed, and everywhere there was a shortage of hull 'bottoms'. *Pacific Enterprise* was urgently required, for cargo carrying, and she hummed with activity. Riveters and welders worked through the night. Each morning turned up an unpainted gusset of new blue steel or a piece of fashioned joinery. Engineers, french polishers and the trades in between worked, bunched together below decks, and she still seemed a long way from putting to sea. At last they came down to paint the 'boot topping', the waterline area of hull plating. This was the last chore before floating. The red was cut in over the black of the topsides following a curvaceous chalk line around her nether parts. And, on that day, the dark blue boiler suits started to pack up their gear prior to leaving. At the same time, a new set of men came on.

Men of a different mould, with drainpipe jeans of a lighter blue and an unslaked, turbulent look about them. The new crew were joining. If only they had known !

Pacific Enterprise was lost, three months later. My first fine ship turned the corner too soon rounding Point Reyes in California, and grounded. In a thick sea fog and without radar, bound in for San Francisco on the homeward run, she had misjudged her distance run and went up on a rocky shore at full speed. The crew were unhurt. But the insurers declared her a 'Constructive Total Loss' and she stayed right where she was, ending her days rusting away, as dry as the day we had first seen her.

Before all this happened, fate had begun to take a turn. Three days before the *Enterprise* sailed away on that doomed voyage, a telegram arrived at our temporary lodging, the Missions to Seamen building, in Salford.

'Cadet A Jones,' it announced in Bossy Bottomley's unmistakably lugubrious tones, 'is to proceed to South Hornby Dock, Liverpool, immediately. A berth has become unexpectedly available on board the passenger vessel *Newfoundland*. Report to Captain on arrival.'

* * *

'I'm Jones, sir, the new cadet reporting, they've transferred me from the *Enterprise*.'

The Captain's diminutive figure was swallowed up by an overstuffed chair, and wrapped in the deepest quiet growing out of a rich carpet and heavy hanging drapes. He had hardly stirred as I rapped on his dayroom door-post and pulled aside the curtain. He managed the glimmer of a shark-like smile.

*My first ship, **Newfoundland**.*

– The New Boy –

'So you're the new boy. Go down and find the mate, son, he'll fix you up,' he said.

I did not see him again until we sank the Inistrahull light, together with the rest of Donegal, below the Eastern horizon and the real business of crossing the ocean had begun.

Captain Kenneth Charles, before the cruel stroke that made of him a shadow and robbed him of his speech, was shaped by the harsh demands of the sea into a martinet. A passenger man through and through, he had sailed on the original *Newfoundland* between the wars, and now, in 1949, this spanking new edition of the name. Safety and schedule keeping were his two obsessions, and the ship's bridge the powerbase from which he struggled to reconcile one with the other. A cadet, any cadet, was a perfect foil for his haughty administration. When fog shut down the North Atlantic visibility, or forty foot waves sent the ship into shudders and plate smashing lurches, Captain Charles, always immaculate, spent his days and nights sitting on the chart room settee, his tiny bird-like figure alert and his feet curled under him. While seated thus he indulged his habit of embroidering doilies spread over a little wooden hoop, and testing the cadets orally on their Rule of the Road at Sea. He could recite these parrot fashion and expected us to do the same, a proceeding which aroused some disquiet. If a mistake was made he would put down his sewing and shout above the ship noise,

'No!' in a surprising Yorkshire brogue, and wait for the correct recitation. This was sometimes left for him to contribute.

We left the Officer of the watch outside on the bridge wing, a place where the cadet should properly have been. At least there was some warmth in the chart room. A sly sleep-inducing warmth. The Captain's tests took place in conjunction with a four-hour radar watch. Our set was one of the first commercial versions. Its circular screen sat in a cabinet the size of a bedroom wardrobe and glowed with a luminescent orange. We scanned it for other ships, our only means of seeing them in the murk and would report them, or not, at our peril, calling a halt to our 'examinations.' A boy's tormented eyes would revolve on their stalks following the sweeping trace which paced, like a silent metronome, his rule book recitations.

The war's ending had resulted in Naval men, surplus to requirements, taking up whatever slack there was to be found in the Merchant Service. This resulted in two of our Deck Officers joining as out-of-work corvette Captains. Jack Norwich was the Second Officer, and my leader on the graveyard watch. In this, I was fortunate indeed. It could have been Macfadyen, a large Scot with the humour of the lavatory, who was the First, and took the morning watch from four until eight. But Norrie and I became good mates, as far as a first trip cadet can be mates with a corvette Captain. He was a raconteur of the first class and I, an equally qualified listener. Norrie was built on a tall bony frame with the long chin to go with it, and neatly fitted the bridge windows which were wooden and square, like an old railway carriage, with his jack-knifed elbows. During the night watches he would wedge himself into the window frame, gaze out at the white crested blackness of the sea, and spin yarns of the 'grey funnel line.' By omitting the terrors he made me feel a part of this new sea-going adventure. His stories passed the watch away, and it took a lot to stop him, even when she took a steep roll – a frequent occurrence in calm as well as rough weather – and we slipped from side to side of the bridge by riding the coconut matting and ending in a heap by the wheelhouse door.

Two or three times a watch, the time would come for cocoa, and making rounds.

Although left unspoken, this also gave Norrie some peace, and time to write up the log. The descent to the night pantry took me through the first class passengers' accommodation and lounge. In the small hours these spaces were hushed with the silence of the sleeping, a solid, comforting silence. All that could be heard was a soft slapping of the waves outside, and the comforting creak of beechwood joints as the grand staircase worked to the ship's movements. We were not encouraged to enter the lounge, except on Sundays, when Captain Charles would hold a church service, as long as a parson could be found among the passengers. On these occasions we were very firmly invited to attend, and in our brass buttoned 'number ones' stand at the side of the baby rosewood grand, close to our Captain. But now, on my silent rounds it wanted no permit just to wander. Norrie was well looked after, in any case, by three good Liverpool quartermasters, who took their tricks at the wheel and as lookouts.

There were two more waking souls making up the graveyard watch. Keeping a watch in his tiny pantry, on a row of petulant bells, was Billy Styles the night steward from Wallasey. Upon orders rung, through the night, he would make up, and deliver, his fluffy white sandwiches. For Norrie he mixed a thick cup of watchkeepers' cocoa. Billy was a vintage steward who had, in his day, taken silver service to princes, but now preferred ship nights of solitude. As provider of the Captain's nocturnal cottage cheese, he had no equal. Only he could dig up, at all hours, rolls of the right done-ness and the required number of chives, so that his tenure was assured. The printer, dressed all in black, lurked close by Billy's pantry. A silent Dickensian figure, he could only be seen when taking a break from his print shop. The day's menus for two saloons made a lot of work, starting with seven different breads for breakfast, not the same every day, and ending with a six or seven-course dinner a little more fancy in the first class, than the tourist. And there was, on good days, the ship's newspaper.

– The New Boy –

The bridge watches demanded all our nights and days carved up in equal shares. Three cadets, though sharing one small cabin, saw each other only at hand overs. Except at meal times. These were grand occasions and, in calm weather, attracted every passenger on the lists. The event was announced by a gong played along the alleyways, a summons that emptied them out of their cabin doors like the children of Hamelin. Toothsome odours lay thick on the air. They hurried to their tables and unfurled their napkins.

'Don't forget now,' the more seasoned ones would confide knowingly, 'the price of the meals is part of your ticket,' and would gorge themselves greedily. But others saw meal times as social events. The Captain had his own table at which he punctually appeared, scrubbed to a shine and shedding his bridge face with charm. We three were happier at our own table and out of harm's way. It was enough to be absorbed by the food, even when the saloon was perfumed by fashionable ladies, some of whom travelled alone. In my junior years, older women were as untouchable as the Dresden lady figurines in my mother's china cabinet. But taboos of this kind did not inhibit my two more senior companions. Until it dawned on me in later months, their empty bunks at times when I expected to find them filled were a puzzlement.

The ship's routing took us from Liverpool to St. Johns, Newfoundland, Halifax and Boston, Mass., returning the same way every four weeks. Five days out of Liverpool we made our landfall. The natural harbour of St Johns shut out the Atlantic like a sluice gate. *Newfoundland* glided into the island's placid refuge, startling the sea birds into flight with an impressive blast upon her three-noted siren. This was my first sighting of soil that was not British. The land rose steeply from a pea green sea. The highest levels were brushed with snow, and here and there perched wooden dwellings with painted roofs. With a shrinking heart, it had to be acknowledged home was far away. Here, if he was ever to meld, a young man must lose some of his Englishness, and undergo a little reshaping.

In port, our duties lay, mainly, down the hatches, watching cargo. It was the Company's hope that we might reassure the insurers and ease their premiums against cargo pilferage. Our presence would deter the most acquisitive docker. Before leaving Liverpool, however, I had persuaded myself that this was far from being so. On my first-ever descent, I had observed a mean-looking fellow break open a case of salmon and place a small tin in his jacket, which he then hung in a corner. I moved around the chamber until my back leaned, sleuth-like, against the hanging garment. By feel, I located the tin, which I then removed carefully, and unseen. I hurried up to the boat deck where Norrie was relaxing at mid-afternoon 'smoko', with other Officers, in the lounge. With a flourish I deposited the booty on a small round table where it lay, dully gleaming, among the chinking cups and shortbread biscuits.

Norrie glanced up at me, strangely, I thought. Then he said,

'Better stay out of that hatch for a bit, Jonesey.'

He walked quickly from the room. And, I discovered later, approached my hold in his customary relaxed way. The hatch boss was at his station by the coaming corner, a rolled 'Daily Mirror' in his crane signalling hand. He met Norrie's level look with a silent nod. Nothing was said by either party. The surface of Merseyside labour relations remained unruffled. But here, in St Johns, the men were quite different, bigger and beefier. Their distinguishing garb was heavy plaid lumberjack shirt and jeans, in contrast to the home port dockie, who was, then, still clinging to a shirt, jacket and tie, no matter how greasy. The 'Newfies' spoke an individual English – a kind of patois, as though forever corralled on this island, like the natives of Pitcairn. There was a bluff easiness you could feel comfortable with and I did not snoop for pilfered tins. The turn round in this port, and the next short leg, to Halifax, were brief.

As though it never was, Chebucto Head lay somewhere close to under a curtain of fog. But the shattering grunt of the fog diaphragm had its usual effect. The small bunch of Officers on *Newfoundland*'s bridge jumped, in unison. Fog in the Maritime Provinces was the normal condition, and the grunt expected, but it still ripped the silence of our early arrival in Halifax, making, as it should, a huge alert. The main ice-free port in Eastern Canada and a 'first and last' terminal for its railroad, this port accepted the bulk of our cargo and most of the passengers. And I cried here, with the cold. It was the practise to place across the closed hatchway, at the day's end, steel locking bars, U-sectioned lengths of three metres which were joined by padlock Inevitably, this last minute 'skivvying' job fell to the cadets. The January night was holding temperatures at twenty below freezing. The Bosun was a good man. He came out to help and urge us on. A film of ice had magically interposed itself between the steel and the canvas of the hatch tarpaulin sticking the bars firmly where they sat, and my fingers, which I removed in panic, to the bars. The intense pain of this cold, with the bosun's barked admonitions started a wallow of self pity, and I cried silently, in the dark, tears which cooled to ice. It was all part of the emotional baggage. The additional hamper had come on board with my new clothes, and was being tested.

The rocky outcrops of Halifax were soon forgotten when we met up with man-made concrete at Boston, a city lit up like Christmas, and putting a glow on the sea horizon from twenty miles out. We came to Mystic Wharf in the early hours. The docks were quiet, except for fans in the sea walls of the eating houses, beating away the odours of last night's fish fries. The cluster of downtown skyscrapers gathered in the dawn like a troop of benevolent giants. I was soon to recognise that here was a gentle yet mighty country, which I would come to love more than my own.

– The New Boy –

The smell of boxwood which would always identify Liverpool exports in my memory, evaporated now, as our last pieces of cargo swung over the rail. Return cargoes of a different sort came down to the dock. Carpenters rigged shifting boards and feeders for grain in its natural dusty state. Trains rolled along the quay with strapped loads of lumber. The homeward loading was a low revenue loser, with deficits to be covered, optimistically, by more passengers. But these important survival issues would never trouble the crew's mind. Each and every sailor would consider, at this stage of the voyage, only the nearness of the pay-off.

Officers and cadets were permanently appointed, and their opportunities for disappearing down the gangway as soon as balances of wages were paid were limited, but the ratings were free to do as they wished. Between the three cadets agreement had been reached when one should take leave, each trip. After two voyages on the *Newfoundland*, it was my turn.

The sailor ashore is a different creature. There is a wall around him put there by family affections, which shuts out the sea and all its associations. But it was not staunch enough to fend off Bossy Bottomley's meddlesome intrusion and, after three days at home, the dreaded telegram. It required, with no option, a transfer to another company vessel when next we arrived at Halifax. The ship was *Pacific Stronghold*. She worked the round-the-world trade, New York and back to New York. She never came home, and the cadet would sign on for two years.

Never came home! The phrase struck fear into me, without stopping to consider that I would be relieved, sometime, abroad. One of my more ancient text-books included the puzzling title 'Wrinkles in Navigation'. I felt, now, that I understood that riddle.

There were more tears, this time in the eyes of my mother, as I left with an extra hold-all of tropical whites, and a heart which was forever sinking. An image was starting to form, of a man founded on a boy and the process was unstoppable. At Halifax, there was a bumboat man, a trader whose business was to prey on ship's people and sell them supplies 'on tick.' I joined *Pacific Stronghold* in a new suit of American cut, hugely double breasted in a broad black and white check. I was learning all the time.

Chapter Three

FRANKIE

Bill Scrivens, on the wing of the bridge, gesturing grandly, was showing me round.

'With a top-hat like that,' he declared, 'you'd know her anywhere.' He clearly relished pointing up her stump of a funnel while my eyes wandered over the jerry built form of *Pacific Stronghold*. Already I disliked my new shipmate, the senior of our trio. His rat-like face and sleazy charm spelled trouble. Happily, the top-hat gave Mr.Scrivens some credibility later on in the day. Jutting above the roofs of the Bush Terminals, at Brooklyn, the ship's squat funnel just protruded. It had long ago been cropped in order to pass under a bridge, shortening the original cigarette shaped tube down by half. Then it was capped by a sooty spark-arrester, an unbecoming reel.

The subway train from the city had dumped us in the shadowy streets of the dock area, and we were lost, when that top-hat, lit up by the yellow floods around her boat deck emerged from the jumble of rooftops to guide us like some kindly star.

The evening had got off to a middling start. First, we called at the Club.

The British Apprentices Club lay close to the big liner berths on the West Side, and held open house in a frowsty Manhattan brownstone. A magisterial lady held sway there, and it would have surely been the case that no sailor would ever darken its doors, were it not for Mary Lou, doyenne of the young hostesses. All the way round from Halifax, Bill Scrivens and Dombie, the second of our trio, exchanged reminiscences about Mary Lou, as though they knew her well. As we passed Nantucket, their ardour began to peak. And though still a greenhorn, by the Ambrose lightship I, too, was on tenterhooks. Tonight we would be stepping ashore to see Mary Lou. Scrivens, as senior, would claim her, clearly. We should love her vicariously. But my vision, already up and running, was of a lissom brunette carelessly draping her figure over the furniture, just for me.

But Mary Lou in greeting mode was American, as some say, with a big 'A', a substantial blonde, pretty enough, blue eyed and comfortably encased in a fresh smelling navy blue frock. When she moved, though, there was the dull rustle of rubber, and this quickly killed most of the fantasies tumbling about in my head. We lined up before her.

'Why! Its so long since I *saw* you. Where have you been to, this time? ' she gushed, heroically.

'All the way round, just like before,' Scrivens said, creating anti-climax.

'What? You mean the *worrrld*?' she drawled, breathing in impressively and making the big 'O'.

'New York back to New York,' Bill Scrivens, with a limp wrist, gracefully orbitted his hand.

'That's about it,' Dombie said importantly. Mary Lou's steady blue gaze lighted on me.

'That's Alan. He only just joined.' Bill Scrivens said.

'So pleased to meet you Alan,' she said and looked briskly along our faces. She nodded towards the games room.

'I hope you play pool, guys.' And then she walked away.

Someone spoke of the delights of Times Square lighted up, a treat that no visitor should miss. We rubbernecked the tangle of high neons above Broadway for an hour or more until we were hungry. It was too early to go back on board, so we turned into an overlit eatery. The girl in the sanitized white uniform and squidgy shoes deftly landed our plates piled with waffles dripping maple syrup.

'There y' go,' she said. In that era, the icy protocols of England would have found this egalitarian warmth disarming. To a stranger in a new land, it had a welcoming appeal.

Pacific Stronghold was loading knocked down cars, 'KD's, large American automobiles dismantled then packed into wooden crates about garage size. They were consigned to Manila, Batavia and Shanghai. Simultaneously, she was completing discharge of her inward cargo, tin ingots, rubber, ginger root and tea. New York was the turning point of *Stronghold's* voyage, but her two-year Articles of Agreement, about half completed, required most of her crew to stay on. The top three, or 'Holy Trinity' as Bill Scrivens would have it, might stay longer. Captain, Mate, and Chief

Engineer, older men yellowed by years of salty sun might stay, by preference. The Far East was home to them. In the captain's case, some said, 'he'd be welcome to go there and stay there.' Captain Frank Barsett, 'Frankie' to us, was a peevish man.

'Stay clear of the stiff necked one,' Scrivens said, soon after we sailed, 'Frankie'll get you soon enough.' His allusion to our captain's posture was accurate enough. He suffered with some damage to the spine and an inability (or unwillingness) to twist his neck. When speaking he would half turn his head, thereby tilting his stare towards the deck. This fixation had the effect of reducing a man, in spirit, also, to the deck, thereby endorsing the captain's uncertain authority.

Tommy Bremner, the Mate, would be a Mate all his life. He came from Orkney, smoked a foul pipe which he primed with shreds penknifed from a lump of plug, and, Bill Scrivens assured me, slept with his little round cap on. I rarely saw the Chief, who stayed as invisible as his great steam turbines. These were fine hardy engines despite their conception and build in the hurriedness of war. 'Chiefy' was down there when we sailed, driving our fifteen thousand displacement tons with his six thousand of horse power quietly toiling through their reduction gear boxes. I hardly felt a tremor as we passed outward, sending a whispered plume of funnel smoke across the censorial nose fixed high on the Statue of Liberty.

We turned South towards the Sargasso Sea. For a young sailor of the dreamier sort, these unfolding discoveries sent up high flights of fancy. The jewel like blue of the Sargasso is blotted with rafts of yellow spongy weed, giving rise to legends of sailing ships becalmed and held forever in their grip. We knifed through the weed, at speed. The flat coral islands as we passed sent out the same hot smells that must have greeted Columbus, and at the Windward Passage, I pictured galleons.

Our entry into the canal, at Cristobal, was controlled by electric mules, whose drivers held us in place with heavy cables. But Pilots ordered the ship's progress on board. Panama is one of the few waterways where the pilots, by agreement between Owners and Canal Company take control of the ship away from the Master. This tenuous collaboration gives rise to misunderstandings. It was my job to write up the movement book, but I found myself witness to a melodrama. At Gatun Lake the helm was relieved by Harvey, a muscular sun-browned sailor from Wales, totally tattooed down to the foxes' bush that disappeared into the waistband of his jeans. He walked with a swagger and came shirtless to the bridge, as proud of his pectorals as a shop girl might be of her sloping shoulders. I watched, envying the man's cockiness. Harvey came up, smiling around him and flashing his white teeth.

'G' mornin', Captain,' he piped cheerfully.

Frankie sniffed and kept his eyes down. It was not for him to deny a man's right to come to the wheel, shirtless. That was an established hot weather concession. He just wouldn't look. Harvey took up his stance, grasping the wheel spokes, legs braced and eyes screwed up to the afternoon sun.

'Hard right!' ordered the Pilot. It was hot and clammy up there. He spoke sleepily, quietly. The ship's slow exit from the still brown waters of the lock was accompanied by an unexpected shallow-water sheer, requiring a generous correction. The Pilot waited for Harvey's response.

'Hard right, now!' he repeated, with more urgency. Englishmen were slow to acknowledge, even though they well knew that 'right' means 'starboard' in American.

Harvey had not heard. Pilots mumbled. And it was Harvey's wont to daydream. The pilot glanced, expectantly, at the captain. Frankie unleaned his frame from the forepart and turned to glower at the muscle bound seaman. Tartly, he burst out, 'Hard a *starboard*, man!'

'You don' 'ave to *shout*, Captain,' the sailor observed in the musical accents of the valleys, and putting the wheel down, theatrically, he sent the bows charging for the opposite bank.

'If this man can't do it, we'll get him relieved, Captain,' the pilot ordained.

Meanwhile, an Officer had seized the wheel, overlaying Harvey's arms. The endeavours of both men caused the canal lying ahead to weave about like a Hollywood police chase.

'You don' 'ave to shout, Captain.' The saucy steersman, Harvey, is second from left.

'Get another man up here,' Frankie bawled.

'Midships, midships the wheel, goddamn it!' the pilot cried . He had reached the limit for pilots, never far below the surface, and hurled his portable radio to the deck, where it smashed into many pieces.

Get him off, get that man below!' the captain shouted, 'Second Mate, take the wheel!'.

'You don'...,' Harvey began. But the Second Mate, who was a big man, gently pushed him from the wheel. Harvey, reluctant to leave, began to inveigh in a ripe sailor's style, according all pilots and captains the ancestry of lady dogs. He was fairly well protected by his Union, and the Merchant Shipping Acts of 1894. About all that affronted captains could do was seek the sympathy of their peers, and fire him at the end of the voyage.

We saw only a little of Frankie during the long ocean passages. Habitually disinterested, Frankie washed his hands of us, and delivered us up to the Mate, who got out of us all the sweated labour that he could. This resulted in long dusty days scaling winches, polishing brass, and 'going with Chippie' when ever that old shellback found a filthy job, such as cleaning hold bilges. I resented this. Our contracts required that we be taught the basics of Deck Officer duties, and not the menial jobs that the sailors refused to do.

At sea, we saw the captain only 'on his rounds'. He was required to inspect all crew quarters weekly. Trailing the Mate and sometimes the Bosun, he would strut, each Saturday at eleven, through the galley, storerooms and crew accommodation. He entered our cabins without knocking.

'You look as though you could do with more bread and potatoes, boy,' he might say. Or, 'Keep it up now,' frowning vacantly at my prettily laid out correspondence course workings. These events enlivened the long Pacific passage, until somewhere in that ocean vastness we crossed the Date Line and entered the East. I came to another world. A world disjoined it seemed, forever from our Western half. An earlier scribe noted that, in that coloured eastern half, 'the dawn comes up like thunder'. But every aspect, not just the dawn, appeared to a new boy, equally lurid, powerful and engagingly strange. We loaded rubber at a number of unmarked bays, waiting for first light before we could see to enter. On the shore, kerosene lamps like fireflies lit up the small communities. Wooden barges, their hulls still warm from yesterday's sun, came out to meet us infused with scents from the shore, scents of unknown flora and the sweetish smoke from charcoal burning cooking pots. Their blocks of rubber bales made a resting place for slim brown figures in skimpy shorts who had lain all night, awaiting the start of loading.

— Frankie —

In keeping with printed schedules, we made quick dashes to the larger ports – Hong Kong, Singapore, Manila, Batavia – where we discharged our Stateside cargo.

Six weeks had passed since we had set foot on land, and our normal gait had acquired a heavy plod grown from decks that never ceased to move. Hong Kong provided an exceptional antidote. We moored at the company's godown where everyone drew 'to the hilt' in HK dollars. Our berth lay in Wanchai (which will live in my memory as the greatest concentration of sewer smells in the East) a district offering every distraction, both pure and iniquitous. But we quickly tired of the pushing throngs crowding the streets, and endless shopfronts gleaming with jewelry held little interest for young bachelors. Back at the ship, I turned down offers of a white sharkskin suit, run up in time for sailing, but weakened when a poor looking shoemaker offered to make me stylish leather footwear in a dark wine colour.

'They all creep around like that,' Bill Scrivens declared, eyeing the man's thin cotton shirt, his hairless spindled arms and sunken chest, 'like a gust of wind 'd blow 'em over'. Nodding to himself wisely, he surprised me by adding, in that coaxing way he had, 'why don't you give him a bit of a break ?' Scrivens was smirking to himself with his own secret. A lot of the ship's people had lost things lately, Parker pens and paper money left lying about.

The shoemaker placed a square of white paper on the deck, and seizing my left calf with both hands clumped its foot onto the paper. He drew a soft pencil line around my foot, withdrew the paper, folded it and put it back in his pocket.

'Tomorro', I come,' he smiled, ducking backwards through the curtained doorway. I folded my dollar bills, putting by the exact amount, locking the bundle in my single desk drawer. He returned in the early morning with my shoes, a beautiful pair. The fragrant leather accepted a finger's caress like a piece of baby chamois and was polished to a warm shade of plum. I had not given a thought to my set of small drawer keys. They were similar to all the others, with a little forcing they would permit passage into any drawer, and other keys like them, into mine. This fact dawned on me when ever more feverish thrusting, removing and upturning the drawer, going out of the cabin and coming back in failed to turn up my money. It was most surely gone. And I knew where. Scrivens' cabin faced mine across a narrow carpeted alleyway, each cabin screened off by faded door curtains. He was lying across his bunk fiddling with a brand new short wave radio, an expensive 'Zenith'. He continued to fiddle as I slammed through the doorway.

'Scrivens!' I burst out, 'where's my money?'

The shoemaker watched us, his small black eyes empty. He proffered the shoes.

'Wha', he said, 'Wha?'

'I haven't got your money. Why? Have you lost it?' Bill's face showed serious concern.

'You know good and bloody well I've lost it and I want it back!'

'I don't have any idea what you are talking about,' he said.

The mask had a deflating effect. He had used it before. My urge to grab him by the throat died away. I temporised, weakly.

'What's the use, you bastard, just give it back, will you?'

'I keep tellin' ye. I have not got your money, now just fuck off, will ye?' The staged Scots accent and bluster condemned him.

'There's ways and means, you know,' I muttered. I seized the shoes and brandished them under his nose. I could not prove a thing. I kept the shoes and signed a note on the Agents promising to pay. Scrivens' time was nearly up, and he flew home from Singapore, the next port. I never heard of him again.

Dombie moved up to Senior Cadet. Dombie was a grey character, no real bond ever linked us, but we accepted each other, and the milieu about the half-deck (as it was termed in grander days) improved notably. An unusual replacement for Bill Scrivens arrived on board from Eastern Canada. Lloyd Bugden, a bulky coastal fisherman with wrists like legs of pork. These were covered in scars he was pleased to call 'sea-pups' developed from hauling near-frozen nets. Lloyd was my age, but fully a man.

At about this time, larger ports of the Orient were regulated by remnants of the old colonial rule. But due to the war, new authorities, with power, in smaller places applied their entry laws more arbitrarily. Our ship's progress met with delays, unwelcome in a world where quick turn round time was important. This made trouble for ship's captains. Frankie, now in the middle of his second tour was showing signs of strain. He relied on the crew to assist him in making the voyage speedy and profitable. The day I fouled the topmast halyards with the Quarantine flag did not accord too well with these ideals. The dense yellow flag, proclaiming our freedom from infection, lay ready for hoisting and claiming free pratique, effectively our permission to enter the territory of that small green island. The port officials, laying off in their customs launch, refused to clamber up our Jacob's ladder until that signal was made. At the open steel door to the bond, the purser waited impatiently with cigarettes and whisky on hand, enough to line a Gladstone bag or two.

'Don't take all day with that goddamn flag.' Frankie was tired, I could see.

I skipped away, down from the bridge and three ladders, to the foredeck. But the yellow bundle, soon tight up to the yard, refused to break out. It was furled with a slippery hitch. In theory, the bight worked loose when I jerked the downhaul, and the flag broke out smartly. It stuck fast, and no matter how I subjected the hoist to various tugs and twists remained obstinately fixed. *Pacific Stronghold* lay safely enough, stopped in still water, but Frankie could not wait and paused to glare down between short agitated pacings.

'Get that flag out, damn stupid boy!' The cry rang out along the foredeck and echoed back across the bay from the distant foreshore. Panic was difficult to contain, my fingers a bunch of bananas. The port officials in their launch watched, with interest. Try as I might, the flag would not budge. The solution was clear. The flag was lowered to the deck, unfurled and rehoisted, though with some difficulty, flying stiffly in the wind. Only minutes were lost, and I was pleased enough with the result, but Frankie stumped off into the wheelhouse, muttering unpleasantnesses. This trivial incident had a disproportionate effect. I never wanted to be shouted at. The last time was at junior school. I felt shamed. There were times when I hated the sea service, and one of those times was now! I determined then and there that if I ever got to be captain (up until then, my only *'raison d'etre'*) I would stay forever calm, calm, calm. This self-avowal has never left me but has operated, on occasions, to my disadvantage.

With the final top-off at Penang we continued our circumnavigation. *Stronghold* continued a fifteen knot furrow across the Indian, and into the Red Sea. 1400 miles long, but narrow, this sea, on navigation charts, resembles a discarded sock. Winds flow up and down it, hot and cold in extremes, and bearing the red desert sand – a fine dust which sticks to the rigging, gets into a sailor's hair and discolours the water, giving the sea its name. We came in at the south end known as the 'Gate of Tears' in early January, with a following wind stifling the air around us. Without air-conditioning , and with only one rickety fan, our cabin bunks were wet through, night and day. Then, as we worked to the North under the bluest of skies a new and freshening wind sank down the craggy mountain sides at Sinai. This brought a startling change in temperature and humidity, and our bodies adapted to the temperate world they had known, it seemed, an age ago. Not more than a degree of latitude divided a day when we had swung aloft in bosun's chairs, painting down the great buff coloured masts, hotter than a furnace, from the next when we stayed down, pulling on sweaters before going on deck Lungfulls of real air were a Western luxury. The East became a distant dream.

Back in Brooklyn, I sat on a bale of rubber, down the hold. Longshoremen lunged at the stow with their hooks. The bales had stuck together as a block and they cursed the floury talcum which flew about them in clouds. Long ago, but only weeks, in fact, I had directed a squad of rag-tag women and children who spread the powder to reduce this perennial sticking when loading in the Singapore heat. In the tween decks above, the kegs of stem ginger, still giving off their spicy scent seemed alien, not belonging to this place.

The round the world trade had slackened, and *Pacific Stronghold* was now time-chartered to an Indian concern. On the day we completed in New York we were ordered to Montreal. Railway locomotives were to be loaded, on deck, as that was the only space that would take them, for Bombay. With Lloyd and the sailors I helped shore up the decks from below with great timber baulks, and saw the engines stowed above, lashing them with wire and chains. Lloyd, my Canadian shipmate, and I were now firm friends. He had come to us not by way of usual recruitment, but his own initiative. The Canadian Merchant Service possessed few vessels, and for a fisherman with a hankering for bigger ships, it became necessary to look for a berth in Europe. I helped him to accept, or at least to tolerate, the outlandish traditions that survived on board British ships. Lloyd taught me sailorising jobs. I spent more time messing with rope and wire than in smart seasonal uniforms. Tommy Bremner applauded this. The Company management did not know, and Captain Barsett did not care. In Montreal Lloyd and I had met pretty girls, and we speculated on the run across the Western Ocean how soon we would get letters.

But Lloyd was unhappy with things. He came to me at coffee break one day looking sheepish. Despite his butch bulkiness, on these occasions he took on the look of a guilty child.

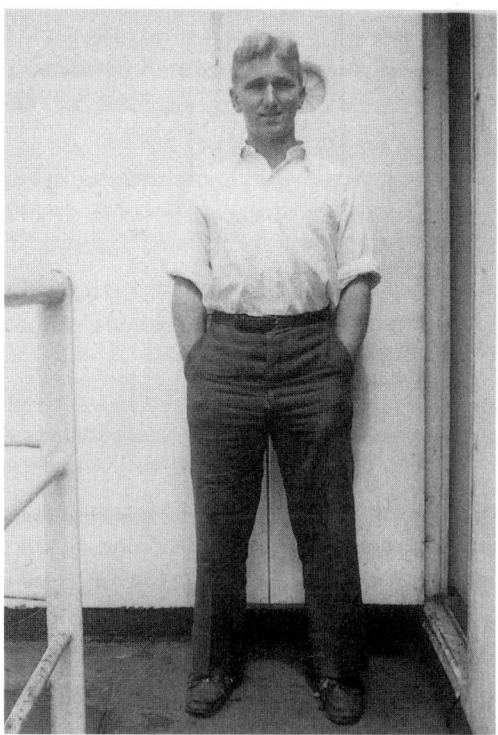

Lloyd had almost fallen in with our rules on uniform.

— Frankie —

'I'm off, then, Alan,' he said.

'What are you on about, Lloyd?' I said.

'It's that damn Frankie of yours.' An angry fire lit up Lloyd's eyes.

'Not *my* Frankie! What's he done now then, Lloyd?' I tried to be sympathetic.

'*He's* done nothin'. *I* just told him he could stuff it. I've had it with wearing them fancy blue pants!'

'So what happened?'

'I guess I'm getting off. *He* said at the next convenient port.'

Lloyd had almost fallen in with our strict rules on uniform. Grudgingly, he had managed a doubtful compromise by coming down to the saloon in navy blue trousers with white open necked shirt. That day, at breakfast, with the trousers in the wash, he had risked a pair of blue jeans patched at the knee. The subsequent interview with Frankie, according to Lloyd, was briefly concluded. My heart sank when he left. Passing Suez, he took the Agent's boat away, ashore, to await the first available flight.

One man less of a crew had little effect on India. It overwhelmed us, it seemed, soaked us up leaving nothing to show we had been. In a country of 600 million souls and 180 languages this should not have surprised us. Bombay docks were a faithful copy of Britain's Victorian excavations. We berthed in a system of knuckled basins and quays that might have been Liverpool's. The streets of the city presented a different picture, however, with most piteous poverty visible everywhere. Sidewalks were crowded with lame or disfigured beggars crying for the smallest anna coin. Children followed us in gangs chanting, repeatedly, 'No mama no papa backshish sahib,' the traditional and profitable formula, but I found it hard to disbelieve them. These sights drove us from the streets, not only because of their obstructing physical presence, but also because of our perceived superior status. Strange feelings of guilt overtook us, as though we stood responsible for the plunders of our ancestors.

The cargo was worked by twelve gangs of dock labour, each gang putting up sixteen men. But as the ship possessed eight sets of gear, only that number of gangs could be accommodated. The excess men sought out a shaded corner of the deck where they slept in their ragged dhotis until called to replace the others. The night duty in this port fell to me. During an early morning patrol, I was confronted at the gangway by a young Hindu woman with a baby in a filthy swaddling band clutched to her breast. She held out a thin arm, beseechingly mute. I still had for supper a sad jam sandwich wrapped, by the second cook, in greaseproof paper. This I gladly gave her. She seized it gratefully and disappeared down the dock.

'What circumstance had allowed this inequality to grow?' I put the question to the ornate architectural extravagances of the port. But no answer came. India was one huge riddle. If the imagination was stretched, I thought, then it might see India as the firstborn country of the Earth deserving the kind of respect a worn out old patriarch might command, so who would deny it? Away from the city, a timeless tranquility prevailed, and each misty sunrise on the Hooghly river, as we worked our way up to Calcutta, was utterly beautiful.

We loaded bales of jute cloth for the States. The bales were heavy, requiring six men to move them, and the holds echoed with a kind of shanty as the coolies worked up to each heave. The ship was soon down to her marks.

Most of the crew had now served out their two years. Just before sailing, the Agent hurried aboard with the message. The crew would be changed, passing Gibraltar. When Tommy Bremner lumbered down the alleyway at more than a snail's pace, we sensed something unusual.

'They're sending the big silver bird for you laddie, pack your bags, now!'

Even Tommy was excited, we knew that he was packing *his* bags, and from this moment the ship was in a turmoil of anticipation. To fly straight home would be a delight, the plane was an unusual luxury, and there'd be a free night at an hotel thrown in. The three weeks dragged as no others. In the early afternoon we anchored under the shadow of the Rock.

The busy Agent advised that a chartered plane would land that evening with the new crew. We must be ready to leave the hotel and fly out early the following day. The baggage would stay on the barge for the night.

The Purser came along to my door.

'You're wanted in Cappy's Office, Jonesey,' he announced, 'what have you done, now?'

'Well, young man.' Frankie's eyes followed the Agent's movements, as he shuffled papers into a briefcase. 'Well ... The bags have to stay on the barge all night. Yes ... All night. We must have 'em watched. Just needs one good man to sit on 'em through 'til morning, overnight, that is ... you'll agree, I trust ?'

The Agent looked up, regarding me hopefully.

I would do a lot for fame, even if it meant missing my free hotel room.

'Yes, sir'.

'We'll give him a pound, shall we?' said Frankie vaguely, turning to the Agent,

'Yes. Give him a pound, will you?'

Chapter Four

TOMMY AGAIN

The man in the bunk above me, whom I did not know, was eating an orange and I was awakened by the haze. On board the *Princess Beatrix* the cabins were stale, tiny and two tiered. She was not my kind of ship. But on that night, what ships were? Everything was out of sorts and the end of my leave had left me fractious. A long time after the orange, I felt the bump as the little Dutch ferry took the fender and I jumped out so as to be first at the wash basin. I was directed to join *Pacific Ranger* at Rotterdam, by crossing on the Harwich/Hook ferry. I might get in the remaining fifteen months of my sea time with one long voyage.

She was one of the last 'Liberty' ships living on past the expectation of her span, and had come to Wilton's yard in Schiedam for a patch-up. *Pacific Ranger* would have justified her place in history by making a single sustaining voyage, more often than not trans-Atlantic, with the sinews of war stowed below. These utility vessels were reckoned to meet their demise, quite early on, in a meeting with a German U-boat, and with these considerations uppermost were prefabricated in sections, and cobbled together in haste. But many endured the war, in fact they seemed to toughen with age like seasoned concrete. Shipowners recognised a good thing and when offered as war surplus, snapped the ships up. But dangerous faults in the construction showed up from time to time. The *Ranger* was having strengthenings added, intercostal stringers, fitted to her floors. Others like her sailed around with what looked like band-aid strips

– massive straps rivetted around their top strakes to hold them together. They were not pretty ships, their hulls had the body shape of tadpoles.

The ferry disembarked us at first light, and I came to her on a winter's day, at dawning. The flat Dutch cityscape was lit by blue street neons tilting the shadows of the yard cranes into tortured shapes. I hurried on board to find some breakfast. Before I reached the top of the gangway I was pleasantly surprised at the sight of Tommy Bremner's cap unexpectedly bobbing about the foredeck, up at the crack of dawn, as usual. Relief gave a little leap within me. In an extreme of loneliness even Tommy was someone to clutch at. Strange companions, perhaps. My senior by forty years had begun to wear out his imperious hold over me, and to become quite normally human before we left the *Stronghold* a couple of months earlier, a trend we both had recognised. A grudging respect, even a fragile affection, had grown on both sides. This proved it, as my sudden appearance had raised an ice-blue twinkle and through teeth clamped hard upon his cold pipe's stem, a thin smile.

'Well, Chawns, ye've come back to me, then?' His Orcadian holiday had been as happy as mine. Yet that same holiday, I knew, was an episode which he managed to lay to rest somewhere in the catacombs of a dried up soul, which I had none of, yet. It didn't seem to trouble him that here before us blossomed another year out of our lives to share without a home to give us comfort. There was another thing. Sailing with old Tommy offered lean hopes for my officer training, due to his die-hard belief in using cadets as cheap labour. This vouchsafed only my eligibility as an efficient deckhand. Tommy had, latterly, allotted tasks to me that belonged to more senior sailors, as if daring me to refuse them, and I took up the challenge. I was easy meat, as risks were fun. I was soon busy, helping at the side of the shipyard workers.

With the ship alongside for a longish spell of repairs, a new aspect was added to our lives. Regular access to the same slice of shore enabled us to act out a fantasy in which we played daily workers with a regular job, living at home, and rushing out each evening, pleasure-bent. I met Lydia this way. There was a newly launched Flying Angel mission in Rotterdam. *Worcester* boys had always welcomed the symbol for the Missions to Seamen without the scorn which sailors good humouredly reserved for all God workers. My shipmate, Charlie Youngbluth, and I, impecuniously seeking fun, used up our evenings in the Mission playing billiards and meeting men from other flags. On each Saturday a dance was held. The young ladies, all volunteers, were furnished by socially spirited churches in the city. Charlie and I, quite evidently wanting in confidence, were sitting ducks when it came to inviting the ladies' missionary-like zeal. On that first Saturday, the Padre, a tall Englishman, with a Dutch girl on each elbow, had scudded across the newly chalked parquet, like the van of a square-rigged battle squadron running free with the wind abaft the beam.

– Tommie Again –

'I want you boys to meet,' inclining his well mannered head towards the one who turned out to be Charlie's, 'Maria, a constant help to us.'

His quiet unblinking eyes showed that he would brook no denial, as he presented the other lady to me.

'And this is Lydia, with whom we expect you to join in the dance.'

I preferred Charlie's, she was slimmer. But in the Mission a nod of approval from the Padre was as binding as a royal edict. You were stuck with her. It promoted international friendship by breaking the ice, the hummocky no-man's land between boy and girl.

Lydia van der Burg was a broadly built girl, but pretty, with blue eyes and a cupid-bow smile. But wanting to be with her put up a challenge. There was no spark. On Thursdays, as well as Saturdays, now, the Mission put on its dance. Lydia was always there, claiming me, her male companion. In time, of course, it had to work. Lydia, I believed, saw a budding affair of the heart. But the unsure Lothario in me could only dream a misty vision of she and I in a delectable seduction, as idly distracted at its lack of substance as a spaniel chasing tree shadows. Lydia was devoted to English movies and we visited the cinema often. Her everyday smell was healthily fresh, always from the same toilet soap. She wrapped herself in a great chocolate coloured overcoat that shielded us both from the cold winds. In the theatre I would help her off with it, drawing comfort and warmth from the point where our plumpish thighs met. Later, I would cuddle this big girl behind a closed up hot dog stand which lay, whiteishly bleak, on the flat open land close by her parents' apartment block. Chill hands tried to explore, but were rejected.

'Why are you so against it, Lydia?' plaintively, from me.

'Because!'

'Because what?'

'Just because.' And she stood herself away from me like a lioness out of season.

But Lydia was not a cold girl, and soon there were signs that the barriers were coming down. The night of the big American musical proclaimed it. Lydia was nervous, I could see, her hands fluttered without purpose, she cast around from side to side as though looking for something. Fear, so it is said, has its odour, animals are aware and build their mode of attack upon it. A nervous tummy can signal the same. Throughout the heavenly music of Hammerstein, the message from poor Lydia's stomach proclaimed it, overcoming the powdery odours of Lux. And on the yellow tram which rattled us back to the hot dog stand, the cold winter's night put paid to my dreams. Any pretence of love, like the mist clouds of our breathing, vapourised clear away.

Pacific Ranger sailed soon afterwards all fitted out for her voyage. She stopped off at the Surrey Dock in London, there taking on a full load of cars for Long Beach, in

Pacific Ranger leaving Wilmington on the 'pipe run.' The tiny white speck right forward is Tommy's ubiquitous hat (reproduced by kind permission of the Furness Group archives).

California, where we arrived for Christmas Day. In the morning Bill Ellis, the senior of our cadet foursome, handed me a parcel. Lydia had left a gift on board, a little box of handkerchiefs, to be held until the day.

Four similar ships of the Furness line converged, in a timely stream, onto the port of Long Beach from different parts of the world. We were all signed up for the 'Pipe Run'. Far from here, across the Iraqi, Saudi, and Syrian deserts, oil men were projecting bigger and better pipe lines. They would carry the black gold from the fields there to a more accessible terminal on the Mediterranean, at Banias. The pipes were fabricated by a steel company in California and we were to carry them in three loads each, for five ships. The 3 feet diameter tubes, in sections thirty feet long with one nested inside another, weighed nearly three tons. An unusual aspect to the voyage was that putting off points had not been determined exactly. The pipeline was being constructed from both ends to be joined in the middle, thus easing the carriage of the pipes over long distances. This led to some interesting speculation about finding lost ends.

We prepared to load at the Company berth at Wilmington, No. 188. The decks of *Pacific Ranger* became a snarled mess of wire as we rigged five sets of booms to take heavy loads. With dungarees stand-up stiff from the careless mis-direction of graphite grease and fish oil, and hands bloodied by wire snags, we joined the men and toiled, black-boy happy. The booms were set 'batwing' and running wires were doubled to form 'gun tackles', a rig most prone to tangling up. Surprisingly, this did not seem to upset the American longshoremen who drove our neat little steam winches as if they were toy trains. Our voided holds quickly filled. They then came out on deck, with four tiers high of nested pipes, which we then lashed with chains and bottlescrews.

Our destination was declared as Tripoli in the Lebanon. We tramped back across the Atlantic again and through the Mediterranean to anchor off the port close enough at tea-time, to hear but not to heed the muezzin's call from the top of the local mosque.

To the sailor, contending world religions are bound up with land borders, in contrast to the oceans where any deity will suit. Even so, most of our ship's people would have made some sort of friendly acknowledgement of a Christian God. But here, on these aged beaches the whole mess was thrust before us. This coastline, less than three cables distant, had been invested with Crusaders more bloody than the Muslims they would have purified. Their forts still frowned out to seaward, taking us within their sights.

'Was the spirit of this disparity still lurking there?' I had good reason to ask. From my family church in England, where my father was devotedly active, a kindly vicar had addressed a note to the American School in Lebanon, a Christian foundation, suggesting that I might be contacted, no doubt perceiving some small practical spread of the gospel. A boat came out with a pair of earnest Christian youths detailed to take care of me. We drove the dusty road of sun-softened blacktop towards Beirut, then a bustling city made rich by holidaying sheikhs up from Saudi. But there were sights more affecting than gold plated cities, here, by the roadside. Out and into the distant mountains spread the flocks of black tents spilling over with tattered life. This was the first wretched stop-over of the Palestinians who had been forced, or displaced, from their homes in the new Zion's Israel. There is no race or creed should bear this blame, unless there is one who celebrates man's inhumanity. The fight feeds on its own bitterness. In our time the numbers of tents have not diminished and they are swarming still with ever more rebellious life.

Empty holds again as the lightened *Ranger* slid away from the Levant, a sausage shaped balloon. Wooden hatch boards neatly stacked like dominoes, holds open to the sky echoing the swish of wash-down hoses and resounding hammer blows from our Chippie busily repairing broken limber boards. Three hatch cover tarpaulins per hold rolled untidily clear of hot steam pipes in smelly waxen bundles, as we sailed a short hop back to Tchamalti in the Smyrna Gulf to where there were pink-white salt pans lying flat at the feet of Turkey's dry brown mountains.

It was the job of the chartering brokers to work us back to Long Beach for our second load of pipes. All regular cargoes were spoken for by the liner trades, and this resulted in our low freighted contract of sea-salt, in bulk, for delivery in Japan. This would take us back the long way round via Indian Ocean and Pacific.

Japan was rebuilding its industrial strength with any commodity which it might turn into something saleable. Ships with bulk cargoes crowded its harbours like salesmen of surpluses. Liberty ships were ideal for this task, as they possessed a go-anywhere draft and clear unobstructed holds for bulk of any kind. We took on 9550 tons of the rocky crystals which Turkish government workers had stacked ready into huge piles.

The salt had a good shake down. Thirty nine days at sea passed their regular round before we came to Moji, where the salt metamorphosed into hydroplastics. We had broken our passage only at Port Said and Singapore for oil and water. Quantities of the latter were inadequate due to small holding tanks. It was also brackish and sulphurous and quite undrinkable Rationing was enforced simply by pumping up our potable tanks once per day, promising showers taken in sticky salt water for the duration.

The thirty-ninth day saw *Pacific Ranger* take her place in an anchorage crowded with others of her kind. 'Sam' boats from everywhere, it seemed, lay waiting, loaded to their marks. Our turn came, and we entered the port of Moji under a grey soot cloud of chemical waste which pasted most of the skies above the Inland Sea.

It was not long before a small bunch of the *Ranger's* crew threaded their way down the gangway for their first night ashore since Long Beach. With the wary sideways looks of unseasoned visitors, Bob Dearman, Tony Evans and a half dozen sailors and firemen straddled the long road out over desolate areas of reclamation. They hugged the crown, as by the side were perilous monsoon ditches punctuated with tilting telegraph poles, before chancing upon a row of blackened shanties, jerry built from matchwood and shuddering with popular music. Behind unwashed windows, the powdered white faces of the Japanese girls floated like painted balloons at a fantasy carnival. At the sight of the men they crowded to the door, a flimsy sliding partition.

'Hey Johnnie! Where you going?'

'Come inside, we give you good time – hey, you sailormans!'

And, encouraged by the budget priced immediacy, the men, all of them my friends, nonchalantly filed inside. It was three days before we could get them out again. I was appointed by Captain Cook as an emissary to persuade them back when the ship was ready to sail. Strong animal smells and a growth of new beard hung about them. As did the crumpled clothing remaining after they had sold all that they could spare, for a last glass. A few of the older ones with fore-knowledge had ventured out attired in two layers to provide for this eventuality. They would not leave for me, until a small force of uniformed policemen instructed by the Immigration Authority made a showing with short wooden night-sticks.

— Tommie Again —

Three days of a mist-washed North Pacific restored their manhood, and after a further twenty, back at Long Beach, another kind of Immigration squad stood waiting.

A khaki-clad cluster of bigger men had gathered, as if at a cull.

'Everybody stand in line by the door,' one of them said, as they positioned themselves at strategic points throughout the saloon.

'Come through, one by one,' ordered another, 'all hands are required, no exclusions permitted!'

'This is something new, what's it all about?' I asked.

'Short arm inspection!' someone said. 'Just making sure nothing's brought in as they have enough already!' This was accompanied by a few titters, as I passed down the tables.

'Get it out, right where we can see it now,' one of the Officers ordered.

'Oh horror!' I cringed. 'They want me to get my prick out.' I fished for it sheepishly, like something stolen.

'Give it a squeeze,' a big man said, peering down short sightedly, 'O.K! Next!'

'Why me?' I ruminated, invoking an answer of timeless duplicity. There it was, a contagion had crossed the ocean after the wars and who must be made to suffer the 'sin'of it? Was it the black haired nymphets of Nippon or the horny sailors who sustained them? And did the coteries of Californian virgins warrant this degree of evangelical protection?

The next globe-girdling run, a carbon copy of the first, ended eight months after leaving Rotterdam. It was time to go home, but the pay-off still seemed years away. Paradoxically, a little delay would work to my advantage, as my qualifying sea time for Second Mates examination would be served out by prolonging the trip a little, and I was thus made, fatalistically, to wait. Happily the boredom was relieved. We lay at Long Beach again when the news came down. There were enough pipes lying at Tripoli, and we were to steam to the West with our third load, to Basra, in the Persian Gulf. A long passage of fifty days, and a wilderness of North Pacific fogs followed possibly, by typhoons and pirates. With the ocean crossed we would thread through the islands and bunker at Pulo Bukom in the Singapore Strait, continuing on via the Bay of Bengal, the Arabian Sea and the Strait of Hormuz.

Tommy placed three cadets on his four 'til eight watch for the long ocean passages, thereby freeing three sailors for day-work, and we took alternate tricks at the wheel and lookouts. Tommy liked solitude, well distanced from Cadets. His wheelhouse was warm with a wheel of living teak polished to a rich patina by sailors' hands. Not for us, however, that cosy corner with the comforting hum of the gyro to speed the tedium. In any weather verging on temperate Tommy banished us, outside and up a ladder to the

Monkey Island, where we coupled up a cold, dew-dampened brass wheel. We steered by a dead-beat magnetic compass with a yellowing card which wandered all the more unsteadily, in the dark mornings, when we were drowsy. The boredom caused us to sing, at the fullest volume, for the sound had nowhere to go but the high barren sky. Until Tommy's boots rasped on the cast iron outside ladder.

'You need not make it quite so loud, Chawns!' turning and descending without another word.

A generous helping of fog quickly changed this quiet domesticity. In the dense banks that shut down visibility in these latitudes, sometimes for weeks, a wetness invaded the ship, with the pervasive smell of salt, running down our cabin bulkheads and soaking our cretonne chair covers. Risk of collision was always present. Duty lookouts were all but useless, they could not see further than the foremast. And our whistle, sounded as required by regulation, carried only a short way. Passing vessels, of which there were thankfully few, sailed by unseen. It was the prevailing view (but not the official one) that our leisuredly nine knots, on a six thousand mile haul, could not feasibly be reduced more than a token, despite the rules which dictated slow steaming in fog. A danger game akin to Russian roulette was acted out between all the radarless ships. Every four hours our radio operator would tap out in morse the same signal, hopefully with response from others.

'All ships. All ships. All ships. *Pacific Ranger*,' it began, followed by our position, course and speed, 'ships in vicinity please indicate.' Headings, we confidently expected, would then be adjusted to avoid any collision.

Passing south under latitude 30 degrees, conditions improved rendering golden mornings by five, with nothing but flying fish to ruffle the glint of an oily sea. The sun climbed up and shined down on us, it seemed, and spread through the ship's company, so that the people went about their work smiling happily.

That was, until Bob Dearman's unfortunate demise.

Bob Dearman was a bouncy fellow from East Ham born to be a Merchant Seaman. His laugh came before him so that you knew when he was close by. Bob was the leading A.B. on the 12-4 watch, the man we relieved at 4 o'clock in the morning. And Bob, wickedly, fell asleep often, when he should have been looking out, and in the oddest places. On the night in question we could not find him. The Liberty ships were built without a raised forecastle, so that lookouts were hidden from the bridge, even in daylight, by our deck load of pipes rising to twelve feet. There was time lost while we looked for Bob. By the light of a few stars, we searched the open deck. Where would he curl up this time? We examined every nested pipe, each one a cosy cot, without result. A measure of panic began to grow. If Bob had fallen into the sea every minute was vital, our plodding reciprocating engines would drive us further apart. Yet to report him missing would be to give notice of his misdemeanour. Spare watchkeepers rushed through empty cabins, the hospital, even the oily warm corners of the steering gear compartment. The minutes passed. What about the Breasthook? As far forward as one could get, right up in the eyes, was a triangular plate, the very point of the bow, the breasthook, where daring men were known to sit, with their backs gently resting on the jackstaff, the miniature mast from which, in port, we flew a baby house-flag. One slip would pitch him over the side and into the sea at the point where the bow wave curled under the ship's bilge keel. Then we guessed where Bob Dearman was.

Up to the bridge, quickly to tell Tommy. Call the Master. Turn the ship about on a 'Williamson' turn, proved by experts to set the ship on an exact retracing course. Beam out with every deck light and searchlight. Too late now – daylight was cracking the Eastern horizon, so post a lookout at each masthead. And crackle out another message,

'All ships. All ships. All ships. Man overboard in approximate position 19° 40′ North 124° 39′ East. Ships in vicinity please keep sharp lookout. Signed Master, *Pacific Ranger*

Two hours passed, then four, how many hours is enough? And who would ever spot a black tousled head expiring in the slight chop which began to ruffle a dark sea at sunrise? At morning coffee we left the search area and resumed passage. There were no trumpet calls, no solemn goodbyes. Bob's family – he was a bachelor – was informed by the Company office in London. A sadness settled on the ship and we made a display of it, hunching ourselves communally like some great wounded beast, lashing out at any intrusion.

We came at last to the well populated waters of the Persian Gulf and the Shatt-al-Arab. This short waterway marked the confluence of the Euphrates and Tigris, and led us up to Basra. Our sailors viewed it as an historical kind of place. But from the banks ragged young men threw stones at us, landing short, while their noisy Arabic abuse carried far, across the still brown water. We were getting used, by then, to how unpopular the colonising British had become. Yesterday's news had put out an account of an Iranian patriot called Mossadeq who claimed the deposits of the world's oil which happened to lie beneath him, in spite of British Petroleum at Abadan, who had been pumping it up, and distributing it world wide, for years. Waggish counter claims presumed the colonist Xerxes, he of the 500 BC period, to have had first call on the oil. The British, however, were the fashionable bad men of the moment. And the gnome-like Mossadeq demanded, and received, the sort of justice then in fashion. The Brits. were ejected. And the youths threw stones.

As if in pallid acceptance, the British RAF kept a reduced base at Basra, with tidy Nissen huts bordered by blancoed kerbstones, but no planes. We shared their loneliness and exclusion for a few nights of quiet beer drinking, while we put off our third, and last, delivery of pipes.

The decks, now without pipes, took on an unfamiliar look, like a ripe cornfield shorn to stubble, and, our contracts completed, we looked each day for news of our next employment. Rejoicing came, then, and silly behaviour akin to an infant school's, when a dark Pakistani agent hurried aboard with the telegram.

We would sail for Cyprus, there to load bulk pyrites for Rotterdam. After fifteen months we would return to Europe. We might even make it for Christmas. I would see my home again, and, with my sea-time fully served, must think about 'swotting' for college, and the Second Mates exam.

For the first time in months I crept up to the Chart Room, for a trial run in sextant navigation. I may, in a few months, have a stripe on my uniform sleeve and be doing this for real. Reverently, I opened the green baize recess in the chart table, which cradled our chronometer. I lifted the ship's sextant from its polished teakwood box, and made my way out to the wing, there to shoot the sun and fix a line of position. It was Sunday, a day we set aside for this sort of thing. The sparkling conditions were ideal, as we steamed South-West with the mountains of Yemen up to the North. The captain, with Tommy, occupied the wing engaging in a post-breakfast parley. Cadets in clean clothes were an uncommon sight upon his bridge, and George was quick to jump, but, instead, high amusement spread across his face. First he, then Tommy, chuckled with superior glee.

'What have we here, Mr.Bremner,' George addressed the air, loudly, 'another Vasco da Gama if I am not mistaken!'

'Aye. Just let us know where we are, young Chawns,' Tommy attempted a snicker, 'when you find us.'

Pink faced, I pretended I had the sun in my mirror, fiddled with the micrometer, and dived below.

'Better, perhaps, to wait until I get to college, and learn the business from scratch,' my senses told me.

Icy December winds sank down as far as Suez, and lifted the sandy banks into presentient whirls. Europe had prepared a harsh winter, especially, it seemed, for us. Atlantic depressions were extending their trailing fronts well down into the Med. Our loading berth at Karavostasi on the North Cyprus coast lay at the head of a bay whose open arms were weathered into a welcome towards the North-West. For that is where the gales came from, and no sooner had we dropped anchor than a wind-driven drama took place. Two small Italian vessels, lightship, and riding uneasily, dragged their anchors to become entangled in one another's chains and unable to use their engines, until one of them slipped and steamed out as well as he was able, with all gear flying.

The other did the same, but with three gangs of local labour still on board to work the cargo, and whose families thought they were lost and drowned. Our affliction was to wait. No barges could be loaded. We passed a comfortless Christmas straining at our single anchor, and, well into January, sailed from there in the fullest gale. The weather systems showed no let-up, buffeting the whole of Europe. And, it seemed, because we were on our way home, they continued, blowing the clouds into straight lines at every Cape. The *Ranger* was never a frisky ship. But even the dullest vessel will ham it up, like a canny dray horse, when put upon by extreme pay-loads. Pyrites are overly heavy by volume. Small piles of the stuff barely covered the bottom of each hold, lowering to an impossible degree our centre of gravity. Our pendulum swing became thereby violent and dangerous. As each sea inclined the ship she snapped stiffly back upright like a soldier's salute. Meals were better taken with one hand clutched to an anchored table leg. Movable objects slid and stuck in lost-forever corners. Our blunted bows gave the seas as good as they got, but our speed was sadly reduced.

'Won't be much of a homecoming, Mr.Bremner,' I ventured, as we battled by Lisbon, 'likely as not it'll be next Christmas when this old thing gets there.'

Not even foul weather, however, could cap our excitement. We could not sleep or eat, infected by a feverish condition known as 'the Channels'. This indisposition never failed to appear when homecoming and pay-off approached. The longer the voyage, the more intense it became.

Reflections on this time are best recalled by extracts from a 'Cadets Journal', entered in 1952.

'January 28th. Entered channel yesterday. Why does the awkward Englishman refer to *'Ile d'Ouessant'* as Ushant? Passed Dover unseeing and unseen. Weather foul. A North Sea day with a nasty swell. The *Ranger* is rolling violently, in sync. with the waves.

Wheelhouse faces are crabbed. Our captain, George, with a liverish tint to his jowl peers out for the occasional light on regular channel marking buoys. Tommy doesn't even try to light his pipe, but clings onto the safety rail with two hands. I am doing my level best at the wheel.

'But, Captain – she's steering like a pig!' This comes from me, in answer to George who is casting black looks over his shoulder. With each wavecrest the ship's head falls off a full compass point. I cannot correct this.

'Just meet her before the next one comes', he grouses critically. This elicits a choleric correction from me, as I jerk at the wheel. The Captain lifts up his nose and looks at Tommy who comes over to stand at my side, steadying his heavy frame on the soft iron correcting sphere bracketed onto my binnacle.

There is anger in the air. Another lurch. Tommy looses grip, sprawls across wheelhouse deck. Captain picks Tommy up. An angrier silence follows. The North Sea waters turned from gray to brown, getting muddier as we sailed into shoaler areas. And, as we approached the Maas pilot, the wave-heights were broken by their friction with the ground. By some miracle, in minutes, the ship steadied up. And so did the spirit of the people, suddenly happy.'

New contact with land, albeit the old docks in Rotterdam, acted as a tonic. Once more, tables and chairs rested on a stationary floor. And the lifeless smell of spindrift had transformed into great gulps of deliciously strange industrial smoke.

Our bags packed and ready to go. Tommy is most pleasant. 'You'll make a fine officer one day, Chawns, come back here with me, will you?' George wrote me a glowing testimonial. Life on the old *Ranger* wasn't half bad.

Chapter Five

IT WAS MY WATCH

The Straits of Bab el Mandeb, and the choppy green seas which gave life to them would never change, their studded rocks had threatened Sinbad. But I had changed a lot. Guarding the Red Sea gate, Perim Island lay as I had last seen it, fossilised flat and brown. But I, standing splendidly upon that white ship's bridge, wore brand new epaulettes, each shoulder bearing a single gold stripe. I had crossed the great divide between masses and bosses, or so I believed at the time. No one had helped me bridge this mystifying separation and I was spectacularly unsure of myself when it came to ordering people about. I fell back on parrot-like command passwords, a sort of code in that seasoned discipline of the navigation bridge.

But, just for now, centrally placed at the wheelhouse window, I commanded all that I could see, for the space of a four hour watch.

All the work as a student at the King Edward VII College was bearing fruit. Life had turned its kindly face toward me. Cable and Wireless Marine paid a little more than most, £34 per month would buy me Chester Barrie suits and all the junketing a young bachelor could assimilate. This came after three months of very short commons. All cadets, at the end of their served time are granted three months of study leave with pay, that is – cadet's pay. This was never enough to cover expenses, and it was as final as a shipowner's last word. For a student who failed the Second Mate's exam., the message was,

' Back to sea, young man, and earn enough to try again.'

This no-nonsense treatment had the desired effect. We slogged our way through whole books of unwanted knowledge which filled our heads, never to be used again. A week of examinations drained away the worthwhile bits, leaving most of us pretty much back where we started.

The moment still savoured. Just one month ago, with knocking knees, we had sidled along to the dismal Board of Trade building on Dock Street, for the exam. results. Divine Dock Street! A good number of us found our names listed as having passed. The clerk awarded us each a slip of paper confirming this. My 'ticket,' a folding parchment with a shiny black board of a cover, gold embossed and inscribed in copperplate, would follow in the mail. We victors (I never knew what happened to the others) crowded the top deck of a No.15 bus, drunk on the effects of success laced with a single half of bitter quickly quaffed at 'The Grapes', and chorusing 'Jerusalem.' Transported with glee we travelled the length of the Commercial Road, back to our residence at 'Jack's Palace.'

Fortunately (for me), officers of my new qualification were in short supply. Throughout the industry companies borrowed men from each other, appointments were made on the spur of a moment, and joining a ship often fell into the category of an old fashioned 'pierhead jump'.

My introduction to the respected firm of Cable & Wireless came near to being one of these, though they would never admit to such stratagems. A brand new cable ship was lying in Plymouth Sound for want of a certificated Fourth Officer. Mr.Collins, the new Personnel Officer at Furness sent me over to the C.& W. building, a massive edifice on the Embankment.

'You don't have to stay, Jones, just give it three months or so, and we'll bring you home if that is your wish!' What a prospect! It just called for a little courage.

I felt less than intrepid, however, as I waited with all my kit, alone, for a boat, in the drizzling rain, on a Devonport set of stairs as old as Admiral Nelson.

She lay out in the stream, remote and separate, as unapproachable as any lady of refinement. But instead of a conquering spirit, which is what I believed was expected of me, my inner self shrank down, quite daunted.

'Where on earth?' it said, 'would I call forth enough high tone to enter her saloon, and eat a meal with strange new shipmates?'

She was something different. The cable ship *Stanley Angwin* was built on traditional lines, that is to say, the lines on which C.& W. had built their ships for the best part of one hundred years. The nearest thing to her, in my memory, was King Farouk's steam yacht in the harbour at Alexandria. She was small, only 2600 gross tons, white hulled with a yellow funnel, raked (as were the masts) and topped with a cowl. Externally she

*Cable ship **Stanley Angwin**.*

Right forward were three massive bow sheaves.

was a floating anachronism. But on board, things were very different. She was alive with instruments and unusual structures some of which I had never seen.

Right forward, built into the bow were three massive sheaves. When laying or repairing telegraph cable this was led over the sheaves and onto a winch with a twelve foot diameter drum. Her holds were cylindrical tanks, into which five hundred miles of cable, – black, snake-like, 1.5 inch diameter stuff were coiled in a 'Flemish cheese'. There was a magic test room where the electricians performed mystifying things with electrodes, and could tell from a Wheatstone bridge at what distance was the break in an undersea cable. The men were called 'electricians,' I suspect, by the more earthly ones among us, but were, in truth, highly qualified scientific officers.

The bridge stretched from side to side – there were no wings. At its centre, her master compass was tiny and egg shaped, where my ships of the more humble kind had been fitted with gyros the size of a garbage bin.

* * *

Things were getting better now, with the first few weeks under my belt. The Red Sea at the 'Gate of Tears' was silver-bright with sun and crested in white horses, noisily tumbled by a well-mannered warm breeze from astern. The maiden voyage of *Stanley Angwin* had left a trail of cocktail parties, from the cable depot at Deptford, to Gibraltar and Malta, with another coming up at Aden. This was customary. Not as committed to saving time and money as the scheduled cargo liners of my experience, this vessel, the latest of her kind, had come to the East on a messiah-like mission to mend any broken cables on her patch, which stretched from Africa to the Singapore Straits. Many cables in this area had been hastily laid by the Japanese at war and were of inferior material. We carried the air of a 'Mr.Fix-It,' which generated an unaffected welcome, running to cocktails, at every C.& W. station en route. The people who manned them had long been putting up with frequent breakdowns, and used any artifice to acquire a few miles of our first class Deptford cable. Shore staff had a way, they said, (I never discovered the method) of putting the final '*coup de grace*' to a doubtful section of cable. Thus, as we hove in sight, or marginally before, a number of Aden–Port Sudan cables mystically broke down. There were lots of them, and *Stanley Angwin* was put to work, to the first honest toil of her life.

We dragged the ocean's floor. A stout three-inch coir-covered wire terminating in a number of patented hooks was lowered to the bottom over the bow sheaves, and our little Mate was suspended from the ship's bow in a bosun's chair. In this way he could feel the tension when we hooked onto the cable, and take the way off the ship with the bow telegraph as the big winch started to pick up a bight of cable. Finding it was rarely achieved on the first trawl, the hooks came up bare, mixing tedium with high expectation. Once it was found, there came splicing on a new piece, searching for the dead end, picking up and 'splice again'.

Positioning was a job for the navigators. Sometimes a buoy was laid, we carried two of these quaint objects suspended on the outboard side of the mainmast shrouds. But when close enough to navigable features on land, such as well-charted mountain peaks, we used these. Surrounding the natural harbour of Aden, the bleak brown mountains rise up at convenient intervals with well-recognised names such as 'Sugarloaf,' or 'Elephant's Back.' Our First Officer, Wiseman, a tall native of Muswell Hill, would lay out the Admiralty chart upon a board, select three of the most suitable peaks and stick pins in them. By a method of triangulation we would trace the ship's path upon the chart. The station pointer was used. My own sextant came to baptism this way. I had spent my last reserves upon this second hand instrument at a Nautical Opticians in Fenchurch Street. It was a weighty version, good in a high wind, but tiring through long sessions.

Every two minutes, Mr. Bushell, the Third, and I, the Fourth, would measure the horizontal sextant angles, he from A to B, and I, from B to C. Wiseman tweaked the micrometer wheels of the station pointer, dotting each period's progress.

There was quiet up there on the open bridge, while we self-importantly shouted the angles. The air of expectancy waiting for our hooks to get a bite was as unobtrusively taut as the watchfulness of a riverside angler. We dragged and dragged again. Wiseman's chart work was important. His mapping of newly laid cable work was traced and submitted to London for published reproductions on Admiralty charts.

I felt for him in his anxiety over this new experience, as the officer shortage which had presented me with my position had also gifted the navigator's job to him. However, I could never like Wiseman. The fellow treated those below him with scorn and rarely passed a civil word with me, the greenhorn new boy.

Captain Lawrence centred himself at the forepart of his wheelhouse, with lips folded, in his practiced stance of waiting. The bridge was a different place when he was there. His large frame seemed to invoke silence, and no one spoke when he was up there. To him, as senior master, had been handed the honour of a flagship's maiden voyage. He had an engaging kindly face whose chief characteristic was a lumpy, wide spread nose, generously landscaped. Upon his upper cheek bones there sprouted white hair in clumps, which he habitually took between thumb and first finger and twirled into a ropemaker's twists.

He watched our slow seeking progress as Wiseman plotted it, and varied our engine speed as required. After a number of fruitless transits over the same ground, he might order in a deep baritone more fitted to the drawing room, reluctantly,

'I s'pose we're obliged to stream your geegaws, now, Anderson.'

The bridge was a different place when Captain Lawrence was up there.

He addressed all officers by their surnames, not in any display of arrogance, but because it was in the tradition of C.& W. to do so, and any other form would have led to embarassment. The 'geegaws', though, he chose to debunk. These were 'new fangled' devices which were put over the stern and streamed behind, sending out an electronic signal which, in ideal conditions might return a 'blip' as the cable was detected. Anderson, the Chief Officer, jumped to obey.

Off the port of Aden, up towards Port Sudan, the water was not too deep, and cable could be lifted quickly; but in oceans far from land, depths of a mile or more made any retrieval take up to four hours with the winch at full speed, an adequate reason, if any were needed, for the many heavy hooks of grotesque and tortured shape which lay ready in the fo'c'sle store. But here at the Red Sea entrance the *Angwin* completed four quick jobs in as many days. This was nothing short of a shake-down cruise, and a friendly greeting back in Aden produced a relaxed air far different from the cut-throat haste of my 'normal' ships, especially when heightened by another invitation to cocktails. This took place at the telegraph station, half way up the mountain.

Showered, and shaved, with all cable mud shed, and neatly presented in clean whites, we quitted the quiet buoy mooring of the *Angwin* and climbed the bare mountain side. High on a flat area of stratum, C.andW. had their station. Domestic staff had rigged fairy lights which hung motionless in the heavy evening air. We met with scented English wives in their summer frocks ushered on by local colonial types – a certain nucleus not necessarily connected with cable telegraphy. We clinked our gin and tonics brought to us by barefoot Arab boys, and lounged under an immensity of violet sky and stars.

In this unhurried way, we pushed our progress eastward, via Colombo and Penang to Singapore where, in Keppel Harbour we were to make our base.

The cable ship, in port, is a ship of limited workload, a ship of leisure. On board, the *Angwin*'s decks acquired the 'piped down' look of a visiting naval vessel. Officers took alternate duty as Officer-of-the-Day with not much else to do but stroll the scrubbed deck planking, and monitor the telexes for the awakening summons to make haste towards the latest cable breakdown.

The ship's routine, as a matter of course, continued unbroken. Meals were a delight, the Company unstinting in its allocation of food allowances and the Chinese cooks taking pride in a pursuit of excellence. Even the potatoes were sorted before making the pot, so that all were the same size, resembling a golf ball.

In keeping with her pseudo naval style, the *Angwin* kept a wardroom. All social drinking was done here. And in keeping with an old tradition, as junior officer it fell to me to pour the Captain's 'pink 'un.' Each lunchtime this pageant was repeated. The room was a pleasant one, well lit with ship's-side windows, and bulkheads finished in panels of attractive hardwoods. Officers occupied many of the chairs which lined the sides. We were dressed to a required style, at lunchtime in uniform white shirts and shorts, but for dinner the regulation called for long trousers in duck with epaulettes of rank, and a tight silk band, the black cummerbund, wound two or three times around the middle and tucked in like a turban. The senior men favoured a wider, more generous band bowsed in with buckles. As the captain made his entrance, I would jump up, on the instant. His drink never varied. A long dresser on the forward bulkhead carried the bottles and barman's paraphernalia. The determining ingredient was the quantity of angostura bitters. Into a smudge-free tumbler were shaken four medium sized drops. The glass was then inclined to about forty-five degrees and slowly turned, spreading an oily crimson film of the bitters. Three one-inch cubes of ice followed, very necessary in the Singapore heat. The gin was then poured, a sailor's measure, which I interpreted as a generous pub 'double.' Never did I receive any complaint. This hallowed procedure, it may be pointed out, was established long before the birth of Ian Fleming's curative cocktails, needlessly shaken, and never stirred.

By the time we had recovered from these long, and, it has to be said, unhealthy lunches, it was time to go home, for the Seniors. These gentlemen were fortunate. Their wives had joined them on the station, and they were awarded homes ashore. In old Singapore there were some lovely houses, empire-built in the Victorian style, solid square grey brick residences standing in their own grounds. The verdant gardens surrounding them with juicy looking broad-leafed plants and bougainvillaea were strangely befitting. The Captain, Chief, and Chief Officer enjoyed this privilege. It was the purest encouragement for we juniors to aspire to greater things. In the meantime, most of us searched for any approximation to home. We made do with a more gaudy company, the added colour, as it were, gilding the lack of substance. Closer into the city were the bright lights and places of amusement. One of these was the 'Southern Cabaret', a seedy upstairs meeting room. Rows of golden Corinthian columns were installed in its dark recesses, twined around with Chinese dragons. Cigarette smoke and the smell of cheap perfume hung in the air. That same unchanged air was churned around each night by the sounds of a big band in miniature. Brass wind instruments tarnished to a dull yellow played listlessly off-key, bashing out the fox trots of the period. In a short row of chairs sat chattering a string of dancing girls, 'taxi dancers', (a bunch of tickets cost two or three Singapore dollars,) who would get up and partner you in a short number. The girls were all Chinese, mostly slim as a stick, pretty and dressed in cheongsams split to the thigh. It was here that I met Angelina coming up in the lift, where her charming, conspiratorial wink started the affair. She was a refugee from the terrible internal wars that were tearing China apart. She came from the North, Tientsin, a city proud of its ethnic stock as being the flower of the race. She was certainly one of these, having an attractive heart shaped face with liquid brown almond eyes. She became my companion and guide while I was in Singapore, and we circuited the cinemas, great air conditioned palaces with bookable seats, some of the cocktail bars, and restaurants – just like any young boy and girl, but defiantly. There were many in the Singapore of 1953 who would gladly have forbidden racial mixing of this kind.

 When the call came, the *Angwin* might spend a number of weeks at sea. A telex machine on board would tap out the summons, with the cable fault's approximate position. The officer of the day, zealously and not without a little stagy drama, spread the news. Main engine boilers were ready to steam in no time. We let go everything and steamed for the cable break.

 There were five cables between Singapore and Jakarta, and more running up the strait towards Penang, each one coded as 'Sing/Jak two', etc., and quirkishly, for no reason, a number might 'blow' in sudden succession, effectively extending our activities. The way through the Riouw Strait and into the hot and humid Java Sea became well known to me. In our searches through its deeps we wavered between hemispheres, and the *Angwin* sometimes crossed the equator three or four times in one day.

 I got to recognise some of that sea's denizens, gliding by, nosing and prodding the cable while we lay to a repair at night. This foc'sle watch was often mine. Someone responsible must stay up there, the order ran, in case a strain was put on the splice. Engines must be run at slow to take off any weight. I would take my place at the rail, forward, and peer down at the cable, my only companions under the tropic stars those that moved in the sea. The tropical fish were drawn by powerful searchlights directed at the cable overside, and refracted their flashing colours into delicious shades of blue, turquoise, and green.

Lying to the cable at night represented the closing phase. After the jointing splice had been performed the cable lay stiffly down to the bottom, almost vertically holding the ship in a grip as good as any mooring. It was in the form of a 'bight' with ends leading in opposite directions but now, hoisted clear and hanging, appeared as two parallels lying up and down, over the bow sheaves. Most of the tension was taken off by threeinch rope stoppers twined around each part and turned up on the fo'c'sle bitts. The tricky job of releasing the splice into the sea without a wrenching jerk, was conducted by the Bosun, Serang and Captain. Over time, this had become a quaint ritual. The men stood by, waiting, each equipped with an axe as big as he, the blades sharpened and polished ready, gleaming mirror-like. The captain arrived, in his full tropical whites.

'Ready, Bosun? Ready Serang?' he said.

'Ready, sir, ready sir!'

'One. Two. Three. – Chop!' the captain cried. Two shining blades fell at the same split second upon each rope stopper lying drum taut over wooden blocks. The fraying strands sprung free, leaping in recoil. The loop of cable with the splice in it flipped over the bow and sank into the sea with a final satisfying plop, sounding softly.

In the open sea away from land, before beginning that tedious quest of dragging patent hooks all over the ocean floor, we fixed our position by sextant observation. This would reduce the scope of the area being searched. There was no alternative at that time – satellite navigation systems were something only budding astronauts could dream of. When drawing my new sextant from its box, there had sprung a warming pleasure of ownership. This quickly died away. In the scrimmage that developed at star-time, all of us, the three deck officers, participated. Each sighted his own six stars, with his own sextant. Weight of numbers alone, they said, would narrow down mistakes. But whose result would be first on the table? And which fix would be the most believable? Under the all-seeing eye of the Captain, we aimed high.

Star-time, those few precious minutes at the end of evening twilight – became a painful pantomime. Book knowledge alone would not do and I could not keep pace with the other two, who were seasoned navigators. An untutored novice must work to perfect his sextant handling, just as an apprentice woodworker will master his tools before he puts together a piece of quality furniture. The observations must be concluded before the firm horizon fades. Time is lost searching for the star in a veil of thin cloud or the mistiness of two sextant mirrors through which its image struggles to reflect. Having found it, and measured its sextant altitude, the Greenwich time by chronometer, accurate to the second, must be recorded. This calls for a brisk stride in to the chart room chronometer box, elbowing aside one's similarly burdened colleagues and counting seconds all the way. Six stars for three men totalled eighteen near misses on the way to the chronometer box.

Next come the columns of calculation, one column per star.

Each man sprawls where he can with his almanac and tables, and works up a triangle for each star with its elements put through the haversine formula. Rushing now, keeping abreast, with a jealous eye to the others' progress. The observer lays his position lines on graph paper, six of them, hopefully intersecting at one point, his calculated position.

The star time experience was hallowed with an almost religious mystique. In the way of shipboard affairs, day-to-day routines which a sailor cannot understand may be wrapped up in a sort of magic giving their players a special '*kudos*'. But our celestial navigation was not worthy of it. The risk of mistakes was high. Exactness was rarely achieved. Human error in sextant handling is inevitable, notwithstanding faultless arithmetic.

Everybody's paperwork ended up with a 'cocked hat', an oblique triangle or two, into which he doggedly claimed his position fell, rather like the tail of the donkey pinned on by a blindfolded child. When things went well, our reckonings were all pretty close, that is to say our observed positions lay within one mile of each other, but the greatest honour accorded to the one whose position was divined by Wiseman, the senior of our three, to be the closest. But – things did not always go well, occasionally we disagreed. Wiseman was quite blunt about it. That gentleman, who was equipped with a small round version of a Roman nose, managed to wrinkle it,

'No, Jones, you don't come anywhere near,' he would say, with a superior sneer.

I am sure Captain Lawrence did not overshadow our work area just to see how brilliant we were. More likely he let us alone to our endeavours, as puppies playing, for he would find his cable in the end, by guess or by God despite us, and just let him get on with it. But Wiseman 'strutted and fretted' his hour. And woe betide me, his whipping boy, all set up for slaughter. He was quick to disparage anybody's efforts but his own.

Deep inside me, like half-pulled garden weeds ready to spring anew, black feelings of resentment dogged me during my early sea days. There would come a time when the ways of the sea would fashion my psyche and as the saying has it, 'run in my blood.' I would, in time, become a real sea officer, with 'competence, cheerful resignation, an excellent liver, natural authority, and a hundred other virtues'– this description originates with the sea-saga writer Patrick O'Brien. But he went on to write that the *successful* officer possesses the unusual ability of surviving the dehumanising effects of arbitrary, sometimes capricious, authority. But that time had not yet arrived, I was not yet successful, and I bitterly resented capricious authority. On board a vessel in isolation on the high seas, a man is inflicted with his shipmates for better or worse, and when friction poisons the air, there is no refuge. In my preceding years as a cadet, I shared all of my world with two or three likeminded others. But now, I was a lone agent, with my own territory to protect. The feelings of solitariness were quite frightening.

It was not long before my unwritten contract of 'three months or so' expired. The prospects of the old familiar, the homespun management of Furness Withy plus a free first class passage to Tilbury with the P.& O., not to mention home, thereby ridding myself of Wiseman's company were hard to resist. Itchy feet, on this occasion, did not come into it, and I chose to go. The cable-ship men were pleasant in their goodbyes, Captain Lawrence most of all. And while I awaited the arrival of the P.& O. *Carthage*, the Company, most kindly, put me up in one of their bachelor bungalows with a Chinese house boy who served up the finest pork chop, egg, and green beans I had tasted for a long while. Helpful advice about passenger protocol came from local experiences. One of these concerned dressing for dinner. I did not own the evening regalia worn by my fellow passengers (mostly tea and rubber producers) which then comprised white sharkskin tuxedo, starched shirt front, black bow-tie etc. However, they told me, if I chose to take the first of two sittings in the dining saloon, a lounge suit would do. I therefore proceeded to spend a slice of my pay-off on a suit of pale grey softly shiny gaberdine, fashionable stuff in those times. Fully prepared, not only for that passage, but this way I would look my best for Angelina on our last few evenings together. She was not at all inscrutable as most Chinese, at stressful times, are reputed to be. She was upset to see me go, and showed it. I.also felt the separation acutely.

'I'll be back this way again, Angelina,' I said, lamely, and not knowing.

'How can you say that?' she said, with her own sad smile..

I left her with tears brimming over.

The intermediate liner *Carthage* was a worn out second best. All through the war she worked for the Allies, afterwards getting a facelift, as she was already old. They joked about her, and the P.and O.group generally, regarding her as a fond and straightlaced Auntie. The only competition (there were few developed airline routes) came from the Dutch motorship *Willem Ruys* operating from Batavia, in Netherlands Indonesia, and they sang, of P.and O., to a refrain from 'The Gondoliers',

' We don't like it much and we'd rather travel Dutch, but we've got to travel P. and O...'

But *Carthage* regularly hauled out and home the people who ran the remains of our Empire, in Hong Kong, Singapore, and Bombay. They were mostly planter/growers, and their wives, with a few Government servants added, almost, it seemed, as a condiment to mask the others with some respectability.

The waiters were English and over-hearty, dressed in white duck with blue rope epaulettes, and skilfully passed around tables laid out on the upper deck, outside. They hoisted to an arm's height their silver salvers as they weaved, loaded with post prandial drinks poised. There were the dense green flutes of Creme de Menthe, ruby red Cherry Brandy, golden Drambuie, a palletful of hues, yet towering in their centre a tall rude pint of Black and Tan, my choice of tipple at the time. Night time amusements when all the deck games had been put away and cinema finished, were to dodge between the decks from A to D, exchanging other people's shoes from outside cabin doors, put there for the polishing valet.

A November morning, on crowded Tilbury landing stage, saw passengers with pinched grey faces, unused to cold, and wondering why this great inflated homecoming had fizzled into flatness. Two children, blond and pouting, were by me, trailing on their mother's hand, quietly crying. They longed (so another lady told me) for the knowing breast of their Chinese *amah*.

'They're all the same, spoiled out East, they are.' she sniffed.

Chapter Six

NO ONE BOTHERED WITH NAMES

———

Recovery had been swift. Shiny new merchant ships skidded down the reconstructed German slipways soon after the war's end. They sailed for foreign parts, loaded to the gunwales with the produce of West Germany's lend-lease workshops – also brand new – confounding us, as we were supposed to be the victors. We were still struggling.

We would have changed our vessels for theirs. They started to show up in places where Germany's influence remained strong. Small way-port anchorages, given over to our slightly shabby ships flying the Red Duster, seemed, now, to cold-shoulder us in favour of these swanky new vessels bustling with blonde, bronzed and confident crews from Hamburg, Bremen and Wilhelmshaven.

There was but cold comfort, then, when Furness Withy, who had welcomed me back, gave me a ship that was German – but elderly and badly knocked about. She still carried signs of being sunk by the R.A.F. These immersions had taken place in shallow water – she was tied to a dock – so that the bombers left her squatting on the bottom with her upperworks still above the surface and unharmed. Unharmed, until a little later, when she caught fire, resulting in the destruction of all living accommodation and the navigation bridge.

There was enough sound ship to make something of her, and Furness bought her for a song. She had been built to sail in ice conditions, so that the thickness of the plating was in excess of requirements. The main engine, a highly charged Krupps

Oakmore was German, but old and knocked about (reproduced by kind permission of the Furness Group archives).

diesel, had survived, with still enough power to race the competition. We had to put up with the new cabins. Mine, as third and junior mate was economically squeezed in on the midship line, horsebox-shaped, but smaller. I had one port, looking right forward. We were lined out with tongue and groove, from deck to deckhead, and equipped with the standard hard settee, narrow bunk, and washbasin. Outside, though, she kept her stately lines, with straight up and down funnel and masts, giving an impression of grace and unhasty speed. They named her *Oakmore*, in keeping with other Med. traders of the Furness group, carrying general cargo out, and, when 'inducement offered', currants and raisins home, between U.K. and the Eastern Mediterranean and Black Sea. Twelve passengers boarded at London, for the round trip.

The joining telegram directed me to B shed, West India Dock, regular berth of *Oakmore*. Telegrams brought to the door peremptory and often unpopular messages. A boy on a bike with an orange envelope, what havoc he could cry!

When young, my stomach could not accept sudden changes with equanimity, and although these inner workings were never, if I could help it, made known, a pallor and tenseness showed in my face which were quickly perceived. My mother had a name for it, and on those days when I went down to a new ship, the 'collywobbles' set up their enfilade as I encountered station termini, tube, and taxi to venturing, baggage-laden, up unwelcoming gangways. The docklands of East London, I believed, looked askance at men from the shires. In all that landscape of rambling basins, however, B shed, West India Dock was the one purlieu whose welcome I could lay claim to. Two hundred yards from the dock gate was the residential college where I studied four months previously for Second Mate. The entrance to the dock lay abreast of 'Charlie Brown's', a pub with a reputation, and something of a landmark, even though we always steered clear of it. It was here, then, that I joined *Oakmore*, one day in 1953. There was still the cobbled concourse to cross, a large area forming the 'pen' where dockers offered themselves for daily hire. I found the ship at the third dock basin, booms all swung in to make room for the crane jibs, busily nodding and dipping into her hatches.

It was my watch when we slipped out of the locks and into the London river. I knew that the Trinity House pilot takes over here, and the mud pilot stays at the helm until Gravesend. But where *was* the wheel? At centre spot on the bridge where it should have been, there was nothing but a box on a pedestal. Both pilots regarded me with some amusement. For the 'wheel' was two buttons on top of the box. Push down one for port rudder, the other for starboard.

'You've got to live life the German way, lad,' said George the mud pilot, 'the left hand one'll take you up to soft furnishings, and t'other fetch you down.' But the gear, though old, German, and battered, worked like a dream. She was a comfortable, seasoned old vessel.

When free, and on course for the voyage, everything fell into place, with hardly an order being given, *Oakmore* had cruised the Med. so many times. For the passage to Malta, our first port of call, there were merely a half dozen charts in the top drawer under the chart table. No one else found this surprising. Her charts for the route out and home were a ragged bunch of three dozen or so, with waypoints and destinations known by heart and nearly obliterated by frequent fingering. Ships in my experience had carried, and dipped into for guidance, thirty or forty folios of fifty charts apiece. We might as well have laid down our courses, indelibly, in ink. In fact I think we might have managed, like some Arab *felucca*, to find our way without a chart at all. Later, on my third *Oakmore* trip, after an unusually violent storm, we became lost somewhere between the Libyan coast of Cyrenaica, and the Greek Peloponnese. While tossing about in the wild choppy swell which outlived the wind, in darkness, a dim irregular light, white but orange tinted appeared low on the horizon, flashing ahead. A light we did not recognise.

'That's Sapienza!' our Captain declared, when called to the bridge, and not forgetting the colour and the presentation of this outlandish Greek cape. This Captain, by name Nigel Coulsdon, was a native of the pricier end of Liverpool and the most senior of the Johnston Warren line. Senior enough to inspire respect, and a little awe in the younger people. He was, in fact, a shy and generous man. Big and rosy-faced, he might have been a caricature of the English shipmaster, honest, aloof, and a little precious.

So – by keeping a certain star at different angles on the bow (with a little help from the one dog-eared chart, and a middle-aged compass) we carried each leg, over the Bay, southward, and eastward again for the Straits of Gibraltar. No chance of a mistake, there. Leaving the 'Pillars of Hercules' behind, we were in the Med.

The entrance to the Grand Harbour at Malta is open only during daylight, which called for slow speed during the night preceding, and all the better for it. For the island, washed by the glow of an easterly sun rising, will impress even a sailor's heart. The sea lapping the creeks and entrances at dawn, is flat, green and serene. On each side of the Grand Harbour, ancient fortifications of golden stone rise magnificently from it. Quietly, quietly, with Valetta still sleeping, *Oakmore* made her way in. The entrance is dog-legged and the turn so tight that one wonders how a ship will swing without striking the side. The harbour widens out into a long deep-water basin. The Navy has taken the only berths. A merchantman must proceed to the far end, and without a quay to land on, swing, and put her stern end to the shore, her head held by her two anchors, which she must drop one after the other in a noisy, clanking, running moor, a movement common in Mediterranean ports. All cargo is put off into lighters, after identifying, separating and checking. This is an operation demanding efficent stevedoring, with each lighter having a different objective. A time to ponder, perhaps, the price of a can of beans, in Valetta. Eddie was our noisy master stevedore, who moved his large bulk about the ship at high speed, mopping his face with a large handkerchief, and cajoling each blank-faced gang who stopped to gape up from every hatch. Small boats provided the only access to the shore. These boats, built in a style similar to the gondola, are named, in the strange Maltese overlay of European with Arabic, 'dghaisas.'

The smell of the sun-baked rock cooling, while strands of emerging street lights ushered flocks of multi-coloured buses noisily up into Valetta were enough to lure any sailor.

'Disah! Disah!,' we skipped down to the gangway platform with the echoes of our hails coming back, wetly. Calls unnecessary, however, for there was always a small flotilla of them waiting for hire, idly drifting. They were uniformly the same, propelled by swarthy men standing at the oars – friendly, older men, flat caps in the style of a homely Englishman on all of their heads.

We were not the only ones. It seemed that most of the world's navies had taken liberty. As we had come up to our berth, we passed at least three 'battlewaggons' wearing different national flags. This mixture might have been a fine, egalitarian idea on the ocean sea, but became much more combustible down 'the Gut,' where a fantasy of early inebriation met our eyes.

'And to think we dipped our flag in a crumby salute to *these* bums,' someone close to me said.

'The Gut' was long, straight and narrow. A steeply sloping street. It stretched its cobbled way from the high part of Valetta town down to the harbour berths. The street had been the pleasure ground of sailors since Trafalgar, and was now, with milling 'mateloes' of the world on a binge. The men were in the basic sailor's uniform, with some differences, as the Americans favoured straight trousers rather than bell-bottoms, and a smaller sailor collar. The French preferred a softer cap with a red bobble. The British, as we had always known them, swaggered a little, trailing a challenge. All of them surged about in small phalanxes bouncing off each other and the walls on each side, which were pierced by entrances to beer emporiums, cafes and bars. Some surged up the street, and some down, singing, laughing, being sick, or spoiling for a fight.

Being the only ones in civilian garb, we attracted more than enough attention, and so formed a single file, walking in the shadows. There was a scattering of Maltese policemen in khaki drills, big men, bouncers we concluded, inserted to quell violent brawls. At about the third door down, we found an empty table. Soon, we were compactly cornered by a small group of British tars who harangued us, darkly, about joining the navy.

' Never do it, boy,' their spokesman offered, 'I did and look at me now !'

What we saw appeared wrinkle-free and well fed, no less than highly satisfied. In later years, in my experience, this trait often reappeared in naval men who firmly believed that merchantmen were not fulfilled until they had served with the 'grey funnel' fleet.

Their thoughtful counsels were interrupted by a disturbance from another corner of the room. At their table, four mateloes had found the company of women. Young girls whose carelessly laid-on make-up failed to conceal faces tired and prematurely old. One of these excited the most attention, as she had in fun made herself unavailable to the present company. With a flourish she turned away and raised her skirt, revealing a generous posterior. Across the seat of her pants, in large letters, she had inscribed in ink, 'STOKERS ONLY.'

At the bottom was Bobby's 'Piano Bar.' Bobby, with plenty of mascara, had trouble with his sexuality. But none whatever with a husky tenor delivery. He sang the hits of the time while accompanying himself on an old upright. This was the bright spot before going 'home.'

But the evening did not end, there. Alcohol was its theme, and so it would play itself out. Ben, also, was drunk again. Ben Londis was the Chief Officer on *Oakmore*, a diminutive and liverish little fellow from Bath. He and I were to become firm friends, but when the gin got into him, he was a devil. He had been playing bridge with the passengers, playing badly, and they had politely thrown him out. Now, as we returned, he cornered us in the alleyway with a strong scent of the juniper. We made too much noise coming up, he said. I had not written up the log-book for the whole of this day, he said. Please make sure he got a good call in the morning, *he* had to stay up all night entertaining, though *his* watch had started at four o'clock this morning, etc., etc. He had the most beautifully shaped head of thick rich silver hair, and it was, unusually, tangled and awry. Ben was having 'a bad hair day'. He was no better the next, when he fuzzily heaved up his mud bound anchors, and we set a course for Tripoli.

King Idris ruled Libya for those few years. Foreign armies had stayed over to 'help', lifting the status of Tripoli from a minor port to a sort of military staging post. We carried supplies for the American PX at Wheelus Field, and NAAFI stores for our own battalions. And landed it on a dock operated by Italians, for Mussolini was there first, it was plain to see. Standing guard reproachfully over smelly streets and donkey carts were the triumphal arch and doric columns he had raised to blazon the new Riviera which never came. But the real people of the country were descended from desert dwellers, described, perhaps loosely, as Arabs. Our gangs of Libyan labour were men of the *fellahin* class, greatly impoverished and ill-served by whatever kings, princes or rulers. Regrettably, they did not inspire sympathy as among them were many thieves and we had all suffered losses, either our own, or items of property in our care In the thievery line the main inducement to wealth was scrap brass. Double locks were placed on all storerooms, brass fire nozzles and similar material was safely stored. Even so, a mooring rope disappeared overboard, and brass sounding caps which were screwed in to the deck came loose, (a fellow stood upon them and performed a pirouette) and were gone. Our cargo was open house to them, in particular the cheeses, stowed in slatted wooden crates, were landed with many bite-sized cavities.

We continued our round. By this time we had grown the look of a Mediterranean carrier with untidy decks, cargo dunnage and detritus piled high, booms flying, and a crew tanned olive brown, fulfilled and at peace. In Greece, at Piraeus, we climbed dutifully to the Acropolis. At Istanbul, in the Blue Mosque I was pursued by an angry verger in an Imam's robe who gestured towards my shoes with a shaky finger, until I sheepishly removed them.

Light and empty now, we waited for our homeward cargo. Currants and raisins were not on, we were told, the trade had gone overland. We headed south again, to Egypt.

Our freight fixer always procured something, or else the Baltic 'change would offer a choice of cargoes to bedevil our plans, confuse us, or prolong pay-off day. Sailors took the uncertainty of it to their bosoms like a grudge, the sea lawyers amongst them whipping up their crabbiness. But without it, the voyage (for those bachelors among us) would have become humdrum and lost its spice.

Across the Sahara they were piling up the dead tanks. The military wished to realise the value of broken armour strewn about the dunes since the wartime's desert battles. Thousands of tons of weaponry were being raked up, amassed at dumping grounds, then transported by waterborne craft to our proposed loading basin in Port Said harbour. We were to carry it to disposal points at Barry and Immingham.

Oakmore was the ideal ship. Large enough for almost any load (we had two jumbo derricks to lift the heaviest) yet not too large for the water depths off and within the port. Five hatches for quickness of despatch, and an adequate speed for the shortest possible hire. There were a Colonel and two Majors for calling the stuff forward, and there was, assisting Ben, me to arrange the stowage. Great tanks and tracked vehicles, some refusing to roll, were shipped first then dragged out in to the wings with bull wire and snatch block. Thousands of empty ammo.-boxes would fill out the smaller spaces. That layer was then dunnaged off and stowed over with guns and cannons. I found the work exacting but highly satisfying and quickly became expert at putting a large number of square pegs into an ever decreasing nest of round holes. I made a detailed plan, in black ink, of the stowage for forwarding to the discharge port, forgetting, in my absorption, the need to duplicate many more. Our berth was at buoys away from the shore, but this was no obstacle to our regular bumboat man, self-christened George Robey, who had taught himself a competent Scots burr replete with 'Och, Ayes!' and the ghilly-ghilly man, sporting a fez, who importunely extracted an egg from the ear of any heedless passenger.

Fourteen days long was the passage home, with nothing to occupy us but open sea and sky and distant mountains. A break for Nigel came half way, a forgiveable little strut, and a chance to impress the passengers. Reporting in to the Lloyds signal station at Gibraltar was an old indulgence, useful in its day. The captain came up when approaching the Straits, running the Rock daringly close, so giving the passengers a glimpse, and a frisson, of Gibraltar Bay close to, we suspect, and of him conning, in his brass hat.

'What ship? Where bound?' The light above Europa Point would flash the standard morse challenge. I would have stationed myself, by this time, at the-12 inch signalling lamp on the monkey island. Like Nigel, with unseemly pride (as I had easily passed at signals) I rattled away at the shutter, making more noise than necessary,

'*Oakmore*. Port Said to Immingham. Please report to owners.'

As the spit below the lighthouse swung out of sight, hidden by our stern, we passed into a quiet Atlantic. Quiet in the way of playing patience in solitude with but two cards left to play, rage or sulkiness.

When I came on watch that evening, the sea was like a pond in the park There was no wind forecast to ruffle it, from Lisbon all the way up to Scandinavia. This was a guarantee of sea fog. It crept in from each horizon, and wound down from a clear sky in wispy banks, quickly enfolding us, dripping wet from the mastheads and hiding any of the ship beyond the foremast. We passed through patches of the stuff varying in density. Only the newest ships had radar, *Oakmore* was never so blessed.

Our bible-like code, together with every company regulation since Columbus, made plain that in reduced visibility I must call the Master. But they made no provision for my cry never to be heard.

'Oh, *Captain*! You *will* be making up our fourth again, tonight, *won't* you?'

I had heard this many times. Just like the fog outside, the lady passengers would smother and envelope. And Nigel loved his rubber of bridge too well. As well as his warmly lighted smoke room, the large gin, and the after-dinner cigar.

My watchkeeper, a raw Lancashireman, was only too glad to come down off the lookout and, carrying my quickly pencilled note, indulge himself in a warm-up. He doffed his cap as he entered the passenger saloon, I knew that. But it did not bring the familiar clumping on the inside stairwell. The very act of showing himself, Nigel knew, would acknowledge the need. He might be doomed to peer and listen, hanging over the bridge dodger, for days. So we just carried on – at full speed.

Reduction of speed in fog is absolutely required. Admiralty courts have thundered out this ruling following numerous collisions, which, despite it, have never diminished. The older hands, like Nigel, put the glass to their shuttered eye and kept going.

But there was another factor. Rarely, main engine damage could be caused, when suddenly slowing from normal sea speed, by cracking a cylinder liner. An unpopular remedy could be found by lowering the speed to 'manoeuvering' status. This involved turning out extra men for watchkeeping in the engine room, maintenance work left undone, continuous running of standby pumps, all highly unpopular with the Chief. The easy way out was to leave her on full speed. At least, Nigel had been foresighted enough, before the fog came down, to veer out into the less trafficked lanes.

But I stood, sorry for myself, with my cold wet nose glued to the dodger, eyes impotently peering into the blanket, and alone with my reflections.

'Here was I, the innocent one, fed into the maw of a card game!' At least I might start the automatic fog signal, a prolonged blast every two minutes upon our piercing air whistle. I could be sure that this would spark off one of sleepless Ben's irritable rages. And Wally, the second mate would come up with his head aching and eyes full of sleep.

'So – I'll wait for Nigel to come up,' I told myself, comfortingly.

At this moment I saw it. A large, getting larger, black shape came looming out. A ship on an opposite course, like me not making the prescribed fog signal. For a second or two, I remained rooted, unable to move. It missed us, whisked past in a second. I jumped, unsteadily – for my legs were shaking uncontrollably, to the engine telegraph, an old manual version that jangled, louder than a set of church bells, down and through the ship, and stopped the engines. And I started the whistle. The noise brought Nigel up. Hands in pockets, unperturbed, and with his cheeks sucked in in a soundless whistle, he looked up into the blanked off sky.

'We have a little of the grey stuff, then?' he commented, amiably.

While I told him of my recent experience, he listened with sympathy, but made no comment. From that moment he ate all his meals on the bridge and took catnaps on the chart room sofa.

We made our way to Immingham, on slow speed, feeling our way, by sound. Each lightship, and shoal-marking buoy from the Goodwins to the Haisboro' Channel, off Cromer, had its own identifying siren, horn, whistle or diaphragm. At times Nigel and I stopped the ship, disputing amicably about which side the sound came from, flirting with disaster, a sort of Russian roulette.

Home every eight weeks! *Oakmore* had added something new to my seafaring, an element of comfort to the job which had not been there before. At each arrival in England a full set of reliefs came down, and we proceeded home for earned leave, short but inevitably sweet, until a recall telegram fell on the mat. Little Ben, Wally and I all had our homes in Gloucestershire, and often travelled together. We visited each other, knew the families, and I found, for a time, a girl friend who waited. *Oakmore* has always, thereby, raised new reflections, given a viewpoint slightly skewed and all the more valuable for it.

I finished off my sea time for the Mates' exam. there, after a few more trips for Sahara scrap. In doing so, I formed a best friendship with a young arab stevedore who helped me to load, ably and willingly. This association lasted, as I was to meet him in later years on other ships, and was a friendship made all the more strong because we each knew that differences of colour, dress, custom and the quirkiest 'lingo' under the sun, could be bridged easily when there was but one problem to be overcome together. I called him 'Ahmed', because the name suited, and he had one for me, no doubt, as we were never introduced. In those times, no one bothered with names.

Chapter Seven

A JOLLY GAY CAPTAIN

It was nothing but a hankering after power and glory. Yet my odd request had been received quite favourably. A vagrant spirit within me had insisted that I must acquire the sea officer's highest distinction. The Merchant Navy's commonplace grades for Deck Officers were Second Mate, followed by Mate, and finally Master. But the spirit had decreed that I must sit for Extra Master, a sort of maritime BSc., straight after the Masters' exam.

I called by Furness House with my idea. I requested that they might send me to a slow-going ship, one which would dawdle her way around on long voyages of little importance and abundant quiet. Then, with monk-like devotion, in the long hours between my day and night watches, I would cram away incredible quantities of knowledge. The company accepted, with enthusiasm. *Welsh Prince* was another of the Furness tramps which sailed on long unpopular voyages as open-ended as a mystery tour, and, as a result had difficulty in keeping any officers at all.

I had, on leaving *Oakmore* passed the examination for my Mates' certificate. The written part presented no difficulty. With confidence, I continued to the orals – the examiner was a nice, mild sort of man. No one could tell me a thing about signals, I believed, as I semaphored a message with flags. I flung the flagsticks about, nonchalantly, and made one careless error. I did not attempt to erase or correct it, *he* would never condemn me for such a trifle.

A Jolly Gay Captain

'Come back in a month's time,' he said, 'you'll have to take that again.'

When it was all over, there followed a promotion to second officer, and my appointment to the *Welsh Prince*, with the hint of a raised eyebrow when I spoke of my ambitions.

'Another one wanting to be captain,' I could hear them saying. This was true. One step nearer made the prospect all the more toothsome. To have a ship of one's own, this was the sole ambition of any deck officer. There was a power and mystique about the job, the sanctuary of the seas endowed it with an autocratic power.

Yet 'autocratic' was never the word with which to paint a picture of Arthur Cooke, newest captain of the *Welsh*. An unassuming, anxious man of bookish manner with small anchors tattooed upon each forearm, I first met him while we were working out of the half-tide basin at Liverpool. I was laying off the courses.

'Second mate, we should go down to 40N and 40W and then across.'

We stood in the stuffy little chart room that lay directly behind the wheelhouse. This small space was to be my workplace for a year or two. In a number of shallow drawers, and above the stairwell, were stacked Admiralty charts, upwards of 2000 of them, in various folios. It was my job to care for them, and navigate world-wide with the aid of their fascinating maps. Captain Cooke was proposing the well-furrowed trans-Atlantic route for underpowered vessels. This way we would evade the most ordered route of storms, and the influence of the eastward setting Gulf stream. It was coming up to Christmas and we were bound for Newport News, Virginia, for a cargo of coal.

Coal again? We often seemed to end up with something dark and dusty. There were 9000 tons of the stuff waiting, to be hauled all the way to Rio de Janeiro. It was not easy to see the practical worth of such a deal. The bills of lading termed it 'Americanised Welsh Coal', that was one reason – it was the quality material for smelting steel. And at Newport News or Norfolk, the price on the world market was cheapest, even if it could have been purchased at some Brazilian working closer to the point of need. In addition, we were a convenient storehouse of supply, for parking at any furnace's door, anywhere. I could never know that 30 years hence I would be part of a ship that carried ten times the quantity, an industry in itself. But I could not help comparing my job with a spritsail barge's man, who, a short fifty years before had carried twenty tons of the black nuggets on a voyage, down my old Thames river, from the likes of Battersea to Ipswich.

Our main engine, a three-legged Doxford diesel, performed splendidly, plopping away without pause, for the whole crossing. When it carried us into Newport News on Christmas Day, we found that we were on notice to commence loading, immediately. This was unfortunate, as the *Welsh* took time to prepare.

– Sea Like A Mirror –

The ports of Hampton Roads are equipped to handle bulk in very large quantities, at speed, upon its arrival by rail from the West Virginia and Kentucky fields. The bogie waggons are hauled up and overturned, shooting their contents into the ship's holds, night and day, without a break for weekends or holidays. The terminal gear is built to endure this treatment, and most loading delays are for the ship's account.

To allow for a free, unimpeded fall of the coal, holds must be stripped of all hatches and beams. This laborious task will occupy the best of crews (on ships of the *Welsh Prince* sort) for eight to ten hours. But we had not the best. In fact, they were the last remaining men on the Federation pool, with a few blacklisted offenders amongst them. Taking an old tramp away at Christmas will not attract the best men, we had to take what we could get. And, now, so soon, we were rueing the day. As they did, loud with their Liverpool invective, for who wants to spend his Christmas Day and half the night stripping hatches? Loading was delayed. Claims of crew ineptitude were mostly unfair, as the ship was of inadequate, unsuitable construction.

The endless search for profit can spread gloom, quite innocently, in this way. A man-island of a ship, after such a claim, may then become infected. The voyage had got off to a bad start.

A seasonal visit from the American Sailors Mission brought small packages – a Christmas gift for everyone. Mine was a bobble hat, in a striking yellow, with a hand knitted scarf to match. And we surely had their prayers. A few weeks later, after a calm and pleasant passage, we were welcomed by the mighty Jesus, arms outspread, high upon his 'Sugarloaf,' as we crept comfortably into the fine old Portuguese harbour at Rio de Janeiro.

A good passage, certainly, but a very slow one. After fuelling at Trinidad, we had passed the mouths of the Amazon. These had put us far behind our reckoned position. When Captain Cooke disbelieved my sextant navigation, I was left in some doubt. But events proved me right, and we had experienced a strong ocean drift, setting against us. But, soon after, Captain Cooke disappeared one day, leaving his gear unpacked, for me to convey up to the hospital. He had paid himself off, with a mental breakdown, and without telling a soul.

The Carnival took us by surprise. Rio, in totality, was revelling in the *Mardi Gras*. Day and night the endless repeat of the *bossa nova* beat a tattoo all through the streets. This music, played with a mesmeric rhythm on trumpets and drums, is unforgettable. The processions kept up their pace for days. Dancers, mostly female, dressed in a minimum of grass skirts and hats of fruit weaved untiringly, drawing every man of the *Welsh*'s crew to the front of the crowded sidelines. I had formed, by this time, a madcap friendship with a shipmate, our Second Engineer. Dick Sansome was from South Shields, an unmade bed of a man with tousled jet black hair, and the glint of the devil in his intensely green eyes. Trouble, in one form or another, came always in his wake. A Brazilian policeman had marched in and sent the ladies away, giving no reason, when, after our first evening's carnival we entertained two ladies in a hotel room. On the following day, the ship was put out to an anchorage, in order to free the berth for another. Dick had no company that evening, for the midnight-to-four anchor watch kept me on board, and he took a boat, by himself.

Sound carried well across the water, despite the clangour of the Carnival, and at about two, in the morning, I heard a loud altercation, some way off, coming from a boat. It was Dick. He had hired a motorboat to bring him back aboard. It was the old trick, tried all over the world. The boatman had stopped half-way, and doubled his hire. There was a lot of shouting. Dick was calling for me. I hurried down to the boat platform, just in time to see Dick take a header into the water, and swim, truly, for his life. The boatman had pulled a knife, circling the aquatic Dick, with the intention of using it. The sight of another sent the boat throttling away, as Dick reached for my succouring hand, gasping.

We were now without a Captain. The company decided to temporarily promote the Mate to Master, and myself, to Mate. 'Mad' McCool was our Mate. Minor eccentricities due mainly to advanced age had gifted him his unfortunate by-name. This big-framed Irishman had seen and done, and eaten, most things. In the early part of the war he had been interned by the Japanese at a camp in Hong Kong. He escaped, walked across China and into Burma to freedom. This was not his first experience of command. On this occasion, he chose to abdicate it, keeping only a 'watching brief' while continuing as mate, for the haul North again, to Baltimore.

I could not hope for any help from 'Mad' McCool, in the affairs of ship's accounting. This was my first experience. Advancing cash to the crew, the wages accounts, and a voyage portage bill as big as a broadsheet newspaper were all the usual duties of the Second Officer. They were, quite rightly, a job for the captain himself, but he hived them off, leaving himself the summarised statement on the back of the bill, the confidential columns where he might find something to his advantage. My workings began with each man's account, his wages less deductions of tax, insurance, union dues, etc. and, of course, his expenses. I soon learned that the man with the smallest balance was the one I liked the least, the trouble maker, the scheming sort. We possessed a few of these. McCardle was one. His origins were uncertain, but he had the thick accents of Merseyside. Wherever about the ship I encountered this fellow I was reminded of Uriah Heep.

McCardle was in the red. I had, in error, advanced him too many cruzeiros at Rio. He would catch up, on paper, but not before the new master came, and there would be red figures on the bill. This was not a disaster, it would be rectified, but it complicated the presentation in a disproportionate way.

'Look here, McCardle,' I said, asking him along to my cabin, 'you're in the red, you know. He smoothed one white hand damply, with the other.

'Yeah. Sorry 'bout that, Second.' he said, with a smirk.

'Well. What I've done is to take two quid from my balance and put it on yours. That'll just put you in the black. But you'll owe it to me.'

'Yeah. Thanksalot, Second,' sagely nodding his head. He did seem strangely grateful. And it was not his fault. Mine, really. But one made running estimates, you could not work out their balance at every draw.

The portage bill was nicely balanced and neatly entered up, in ink, for our new captain, who was waiting on the dock at Baltimore. This put my relations with Bertie Collard on a solid base. We loaded our cargo of concentrates, for Yokohama. It was comforting to have Bertie with us. But there was more to him than met the eye.

Bertie, in the confined space behind the chart table came up to me a little too closely. Bertie laughed too much at my feeble jokes. Bertie praised my work to excess. Bertie was gay.

Unbelievably, I never guessed until the voyage's troubled end, at the Port of London. We had been anchored off the pier at Southend, waiting far too long for the resolution of a dockers' dispute up at the Royal docks. Bertie must have decided to give up and live dangerously, for he invited a boy friend to come and stay aboard, when, for the rest of us, contact with the shore was not permitted.

At that time, though, for the space of a peaceful six week plod across the great Pacific, Bertie had time to settle in, passing his days in affable inertia and strolling about the ship in a set of sweat-soiled whites. A shortish figure, well covered, round and rubber-like, his movements belied his build, for he seemed to glide about the decks, hands in pockets, with his greying hair brushed flat conferring an extra lubricity.

His job would one day be mine. I felt this greedy ambition even more acutely as I watched Bertie's incompetence start to show. My course director at Cardiff College had returned my papers with good marks, and favourable comment. I just could not wait.

In Tokyo Bay there were submarine nets. A boom defence supported them making the narrowest part of the entrance impassable but for a small gap, marked by buoys, which was left open for the usual maritime traffic. This 'gate' had to be taken on the swing while, simultaneously, the ship's head was put on a new course for either Yokohama, Kawasaki, or Chiba.

Any captain will suffer some uneasiness, when, after weeks of landless horizons he comes up to the bridge to find strange territory on every side. Lumps of unfamiliar land approached us with tantalising slowness.

– A Jolly Gay Captain –

Bertie was in a dry-mouthed funk, looking for the gap in the boom, looking for the boom buoy markers, knowing it to be far too soon.

'Can you make 'em out yet, Second Mate? Yes? Wha., wha., where away? '

'There, Captain, fine to port,' I said. I could just make it out, indistinctly peeping up against the overshadowing land. The coloured buoys showed up a moment later, then the configuration started to take on a depth and shape. We came right up to it. The buoys were almost under our bow.

'Hard a starboard!' called Bertie. He was doing well. Paddy Weadick, the man at the wheel, an old hand, and about the steadiest of our lot down aft, put the wheel hard over.

The blunt bows sluggishly started to swing, so slow to start, much more difficult to stop. We cleared the boom entrance, swinging as we went. And swinging some more. Bertie stood, so surprised by the juggernaut in his hands, that he could not dredge up what to do next. A precious second or two ticked by. She was still swinging, too far and too fast. Soon she would be in danger of ramming the boom. It was just too nerve racking for me. I moved back to a position near Weadick's stand.

'Meet her, Paddy,' I cried,'midships the wheel and steady up!'

'Aye, aye.' Paddy replied, perplexed. He scanned my face and then Bertie's before putting the wheel the other way, timidly at first, then with some firmness.

We steadied up, at last, on course for Yokohama. The word soon spread of poor Bertie's conduct on the bridge. Our crew, with more than its fair share of delinquents, had an instinctive feeling for such things. Soon after we moored at a coal-black pier in the industrial dockland of Kawasaki, most of these men wandered off and holed themselves up in the nearest convenient bar, with every intemtion of staying there. Ships' crews, while in Japanese ports followed, as a matter of right, this Bacchanalian course, but the more decent ones, of which we had only a sprinkling, put up a token showing, on board, during the day. The lack of manpower soon showed.

Officers were not greatly different. They chose the better bars in town. And, they did return, for work. It was my night duty, so that I was privileged to watch them return. They brought with them some young ladies, and I noticed that there was one in excess. They sat around in the conviviality of the smoke room, and then retired to their cabins in pairs, leaving behind little Kaiko, a twenty year old in a little yellow dress, and a wallflower, if ever there was one. She could not leave now. There was no taxi until morning. I felt responsibility for her. I ushered her to my cabin, closed the door and locked it from the outside, leaving her to sleep, and later, at six am, seeing all the ladies away. We joined them all, the following night, in the same bar. Kaiko came up to me with a smile and a gentle peck on the cheek.

'Ayan, Ayan, you very gentleman,' she said, not just once. I felt that I was good, and there is nothing so bad as that.

Back aft in the crew quarters, things were not so starry-eyed. 'Mad' McCool went along in the morning to the Bosun, a decent sober fellow from London.

'Let's swing all the boom gear in, Bos.' he said, 'it will make the sailing more easy.'

'Can't do it, Chief. All the men are adrift.'

This was not their first disagreement. The men were just about unmanageable. It had been worsening all voyage. Bad men brought out the evil in 'Mad' McCool.

'Alright. Bos., we've been through all this before. I'll log you for wilfully disobeying an order.' The 'logging' entailed an entry, by the Captain, in the Official Log, and a fine. Loud shouting accompanied our Bosun, trailing the Mate along the deck. The Mate closed his ears, even though he knew quite well that the Bosun could not perform the job alone.

' I'll get you for this, Bosun,' he promised.

The bosun snapped. He swung a fist, connecting with McCool's face. McCool hit back. I watched them roll under the lifeboat davits, grappling and bloodied, punching, until reason prevailed. My attempts to separate them were not successful.

The angry miasma lasted. Long after we got our men back and sailed away eastward, across the foggy North Pacific. It encouraged McCardle in Vancouver, to jump ship, and another with him. With our homeward load of timber and forest products it stayed festering, through the Panama and into the Surrey Commercial Dock, after again waiting off Southend with Bertie, and his friend, for the dockers' labour dispute to end.

A short spell of home leave followed. But the anger followed me. I was called to the Tower Hill magistrates' court, as a witness at the trial of our Bosun, charged with wilfully disobeying an order, and striking an officer. I tried to tell the lawyer what an upright man he really was. But they sent him down for forty days.

Professor Clough-Smith at Cardiff had returned to me a set of my brainstorming trigonometrical identities. 'This is good work, some of these are quite hard,' he had noted in the margin. I would suffer the *Welsh*, until college. This was a sensible choice in every way, for the ship, by any yardstick was interesting, and despite her shortcomings generated affection, like a warm and worn out pullover.

Poor Bertie had gone, and with him 'Mad' McCool. For this voyage, the Company, aware of the need, had injected fresh blood. The new crew would do as they were told, with good will. A new set of catering staff produced 'passenger boat' menus.

Geoff Lindsay, our captain, was an 'energiser' and just the man for a stale ship, especially now. She was chartered for the round voyage to arctic Siberia. Only in the high summer could we steam up around the North Cape of Norway and into the Kara Sea, by Novaya Zemlya, a place where magnetic compasses cease to function. Up there, where the meridians of longitude converged, we would traverse nearly one fifth of the earth in as many days.

At the mouth of the Yenisei river, the Dudinka pilot clambered up, puffing at his tube cigarette, and, after a full day's run we came to Port Igarka straddling both banks, a litter of shanty cabins built of weathered pinewood trunks. Felt-booted tally girls came out with the lighters, and checked bundles of sawn lumber, as we loaded for Antwerp. No contact with the shore was allowed by the Russian authorities. Armed guards returned Pictorial magazines, such as *Life*, to us, after they were offered to the girls. But the hatch foreman, mysteriously aware of the gin bottle in my cupboard, hauled himself up from time to time, poured two inches into a tumbler, shouted

'Nostroviya!' and chucked it down, neat, in one eye-streaming gasp.

Geoff Lindsay, from Mold, was, when safely ashore at home, an expert with a sewing machine, and ran up dresses for his wife. With the Russians, he made a disarming host, and was taken ashore (the only one permitted) returning with the huge pockets of his bridge-coat bulging with oranges. But Lindsay was wanted for another appointment. After putting our Russian timber ashore at Antwerp, and coasting with us around to Glasgow, he left.

Alfy Wiles, whom nothing troubled, replaced him. Alfy, one of our band of 'Furness Yanks' spoke with a pseudo American drawl. This was not uncommon in men who had spent more time in that country than elsewhere.

'Why,' a mellowed ship's carpenter had once put to me, 'if you could pick up your house and put it in a new location, next to a new pub, why – it'd be a new home, now, wouldn't it, lad ? I dare say it's all the same with these ships of ours.'

We had been conscripted for the Furness B service. The A service was the cream, of course. Six Pacific class vessels covered the company's main liner trade to the Pacific Northwest via Panama, from Manchester and Glasgow. Their names spelt, incompletely, Furness - Fortune, Unity, Reliance, Northwest, Envoy and Stronghold. Furness had agencies and managers at every port from Long Beach to Vancouver, B.C.

This service brought back to Britain forest products, lead and tin, Yakima valley apples, dried fruit, and Californian citrus fruit in season. But the outward payload, Scotch whisky, commanded the highest revenue, and demanded the greatest stewardship. The Pacific boats could not carry enough of it, hence the creation of the B service, and, in its van, the *Welsh Prince*. Whisky from Scotland was highly regarded by the West Coast states. Dockers, longshoremen and ships' crews also displayed a keen interest, and regarded its acquisition as fair game. Each handler, along the precious liquid's way, from Scottish distillery to United States liquor store, found his main duty to be the restraint of pilferers. But the Glasgow jib crane driver who slams a sling load of whisky against the hatch coaming, by accident, and every docker who pulls out from nowhere a galvanised mug with which to catch the golden drops released thereby, can not, in practical terms, be put up for punishment. And wobbly men climbing out at the end of the day, risking broken heads, would always be protected by their kind. Officers were doubled, and attempts inexpertly made to tally in the quantities. Two watchmen per hatch were engaged.

The bottles were packed in wooden cases (pallets had not yet put in an appearance) and stowed to about twelve high, with space to cover with more cargo, usually unpacked cars, rolled in, on top. Every ship loaded a total of 50/60,000 cases. Each loading day's end brought a search for 'stashed' bottles, easy to find as hiding places were repeated, from ship to ship. A few of these were intact, ready for taking home, others had already been broached, and there were men, past praying for, who, having downed their few shots, would urinate into the bottle's remainder, on the principle that if he could not have it, a curse be on those who, unsuspectingly, could, and did. This proceedure, with some variations, was repeated at every port. In California, crew would take along their cold beer to the thirsty longshoreman in his hold, exchanging same for a bottle, or two. This would result in a crew too drunk to batten down and sail, so that it was left to we few officers to perform the task; and upon our carpeted cabin decks a forest of bottles, the fruits of a last search, put to sea with us, miniatures to demi-johns, in every famous label. These were dumped overboard, as, with their consignees unknown, Customs would forbid their being landed at a subsequent port. Dick, my engine room companion, and I, when taking a tipple, always selected gin and tonic, the safest proof of non-association. This drink was uncommon, on the coast.

Dick was an engineer, and as such was not a part of the deck department and our cargo experiences. But still a powerful force for good, as it was he who first had the notion of a party. Dick had, though, been lying low for some time. We had arrived at Long Beach, amply announced, and on file with the U.S. intelligence services. Our recent Russian visit called for rigorous examination. Coast Guard men brought geiger counters, gauging each load of landed cargo for nuclear contamination, and all of us were put through a personal interview. I told them all I knew, which was very little. But Dick, I subsequently heard, with his delight in story-telling, had engaged their riveted interest. It all took some time to unravel. Dick emerged, as they say, 'with egg on his face.' The United States was going through one of its unlovely periods, a senator named McCarthy had labelled many independent Hollywood stars as Communist, and un-American. Despite this, my familiarity with the coast continued to grow, as did my respect and affection for the people and the country. It has stayed with me, always

Dick was soon restored, full of confidence. And full of new ideas.

– A Jolly Gay Captain –

'Let's have a party!' had put the ship on its mettle.

We had landed the last of our outward cargo, and sailed to the head of a heavily wooded inlet on the west coast of Vancouver island, arriving at Port Alberni, where the air was sweet with the scent of cut cedar. A Japanese charterer had taken us on. *Kawasaki Kissen Kaisha* had turned up a cargo of timber. We were to carry it to South African ports. It was a voyage charter, and they had repainted our funnel in the Japanese company colours, a red band, superimposed with a huge white K. Dick was sitting in my cabin.

'A party is just what we all need,' he said, 'let's call the nurses' home, there must be *some* of 'em willing enough.' Twelve came down, to a smoke room lighted with coloured bulbs and draped with flags, seductively. The cook had produced a pile of canapes, and, of course, there was no limit to the drinks, and recorded music enough to last a long evening. To Dick's credit, it all went off very well. The boys behaved with rectitude, at least for that part of the evening given to public display. The girls were sweet, and asked us back to the nurse's home two or three nights later.

We topped off at Coos Bay, Oregon, sailing then for Cape Town via Panama, a long, long haul, even for the *Welsh*. In addition my studies, I caught up with my chart corrections, damaging my eyes permanently, from the strain of the night-time orange light which so dimly illuminated the chart table.

The South Atlantic spoiled us with trade winds and sunshine. But six months had passed since we were home. Each day, after the noon fix by sextant, as I reckoned our speed and distance run, I counted the miles as putting us that much nearer to a future full of better things. There is not, I believe, a seaman who would tell you differently. The life afloat, though at times no more than a tropic holiday, is an unnatural suspension of a real life, on real land, with one's own real people. Cape Town, Port Elizabeth, East London, Lourenco Marques and Beira slipped by, a merging train of long bustling docksides. Even Dick was losing his grip. By popular demand he had arranged a party with nurses, again, but the girls spoke Afrikaans more readily than English, and the whole thing flopped.

So it happened one day, on which Dick and I, seeking excitement, had scaled a couple of flagposts outside an imposing office building in Port Louis, Mauritius. A cargo of bulk sugar awaited us there. We were killing each other, cowboy style, from the masts, with imitation pistols. A black fellow passed by, amused at our performance.

'Come with me,' he said, 'I'll show you something good.'

Paying for the taxi, and a few rounds of Tiger beer, we found ourselves at a kraal, where, in a little hut, a group of sugar cane cutters, mostly girls, were smoking marijuana. Nothing loath, we joined them. Very shortly after, on the way back, we agreed, there was not much to that stuff, our first experience. I remember well. I reached for my pack of Senior Service, lighting up gratefully.

Bulk sugar came aboard in bags. The gangs had spaced out the hatch boards so leaving a filtering space. They slit the bags, emptying their contents, so filling each hold with the grey brown bulk. The cargo was consigned to a sugar company's refining warehouse, at Greenock. In four weeks we would be there, and on the train home.

But no! Up in Egypt, an overweening soldier was throwing his weight about. Colonel Abdul Nasser had annexed the Suez Canal. The shareholders in Paris and London, and shipowners using the waterway became alarmed. British, French and Israeli forces invaded. The canal was closed. Our homeward voyage was thus lengthened, and in place of the straight run up through the Suez, we were constrained to take the long route back around the Cape. There was one ray of hope. I might-just-get all my sea time in for the Masters' course, at the Cardiff College of Technology.

Chapter Eight

A SLIGHT DISRUPTION

The halls of academia were closed to me, and the clipped and pleasant greens of Sophia Gardens made an adequate substitute, as I dozed. *Deviation and the Deviascope* lay flattened on my chest, open at a difficult page.

This was Cardiff in a warm August and the College of Technology was in recess for the summer 'hols,' breaking up my period of study. The course for the Masters' exam. occupied three months. I had arrived in May, in a hurry, joining a course that was already half-way through. Impatient to start, I decided to risk the disruption and turn the delay to my advantage, to fill in the missing bits by studying during the holiday.

This day I chose a place in the sunlit gardens, within a waft of ranks of roses, lying in the grass and willing myself to read. There was much hard reading to do. Shipmasters' business was veiled in incomprehensible language. Ships 'lost or not lost' and the 'restraints of kings, princes and rulers' were historical terms having little relevance, and, as I pungently offered to my companions, should have been chucked out, long ago.

Deviascope I could live with. It was all about magnetism, and how the earth's field swipes the needles of my compass, how lumps of iron in the ship's structure will deflect it, and how, as in the deviascope, magnets may be laid on a board to compensate. This I could apply myself to. It was part of a paper, and positioning magnets in the orals was an area fraught with failure. But the extended push to Extra Master's which I planned and had studied for, I now learned would require much more than three-month's reading. More like a year.

'You must take a year at sea, first, for the reading bit,' a candidate at the hotel, nearly at the sitting stage, advised me. 'It's recommended. Part A will get your theory done, the economic geography, the oceanography, and all that stuff. Then come ashore for Part B, the maths and science bit. You'll need the proper lectures for that.'

I had not planned adequately, my incautious acts of castle building had run ahead much too fast, I was having doubts about the whole thing. I would need more financing. My two years work on the *Welsh* had not been in vain, it was just that I would need more. A whole lot more. And my affairs were changing more rapidly than life on the oceans could ever have foreseen.

I was boarding at the Cardiff Merchant Navy hotel, and able to visit my parental home, in Gloucester, every two weeks. On these Saturdays I rode the economical bus arriving, first, at that city's New Inn. My two friends, each with his tipple, a Mackesons' and a lager, would be standing at the bar, with my usual pint of bitter under wraps. But there was more than this. There was a girl. This lovely person had first swept into the cocktail bar, and into my life, some weeks earlier, making all eyes turn. She wore a flared dress in a shocking pink with a matching hat, broad brimmed and shaped like an oyster shell. Under it was piled up her glorious chestnut hair. Her elderly father, with bowler and stick, accompanied her, but they separated when he made for the gentleman's bar.

'I'll get to know him, first,' I thought. She was not easy to approach, being under some sort of escort. But she did have a fluffy brown spaniel, good neutral ground, I was not slow to note. I walked Southgate Street, often, wishing to bump into her. My trips up from Cardiff did not slacken.

My papers went in for sitting the exam. in September. This was rash, I knew, but I wanted to be through with it, and I felt lucky. By great good fortune, most of the questions in all six papers, which I had boned up upon so assiduously, came up. And, surprisingly, my fingers overcame the rickety old deviascope which had been rusting away in the Bute Street exam. rooms for decades. I passed for Master (Foreign Going) in that September, 1957. I was 26. This was a fair average for any young man willing to push through his sea-time, and study responsibly. The boys at the New Inn thought me too young, and said so. For them, I produced the document, which impressed them sufficiently with its copper plate, shiny cover and and gold scrolling. But it was true that most people ashore equated the 'ticket' with the job, that the Merchant Service offered instant employment to ship's captains of a tender age. This, of course, was far

The document, black and gold with fancy copperplate.

from the case. It was a matter of 'dead men's shoes.' And the rung above me sustained many, many shoes fitting whole ranks of dismayingly healthy fortyish masters.

I was offered a watchkeeper's post on the Furness luxury liner, Queen of Bermuda. I declined this, as, running from New York to Bermuda, I would not have seen home again for two years. This was all the more important as, with all thought of Extra Masters' now abandoned, I had proposed to my Judy Gray (for so she was called) and was accepted.

Pinemore was a small, near-new ship.

Getting an introduction had not been easy. The cocktail bar at the New Inn was claimed as his domain by Jerry, its redoubtable bar-tender. Jerry maintained the exclusiveness of the place by the simple expedient of freezing out undesirables. At the slightly open door, he stood tall, a slim six feet and gleamingly hairless, wearing with pride a snow-white floor length apron and a caterers' jacket, stiffly starched. Jerry would guard any ladies of good taste, and there was no room for lounge lizards. For an introduction to the lady who always sat on the stool at the end, I had, first, to let him see me and know me. Then, my duty told me, to follow it up with a gift bottle of Canadian Rye.

Then came the offer of a Chief Officer's position on a small, nearly-new ship. The *Pinemore* was one of the Furness group's vessels operating through the Mediterranean, with twelve passengers.

'Exposure!' a man a lot more senior had once propounded, to me, 'a little exposure would do you the world of good!' My new promotion had pushed me, willy-nilly, to the front. Until now the performance of my duties had concerned only myself, and the impersonal trappings of a cargo ship. That had changed, and I was having to measure up to other people. There was a crew of twelve, bosun, carpenter and seamen. You could throw in the firemen and stewards as they were often included. It was up to me to keep good relations with the engineers and catering staff, with the general aim of running the ship smoothly. I was to hire and fire, and give my men voyage-end discharges of Very Good, or Good, or Decline to Report. This last was used extremely rarely, and I never did. We had employed two such on the *Welsh*, only because there were no more men available. The union, with whom we often entered into verbal conflict, defined our proceedures as arbitrary and capricious, which, in truth they were. It was rough, but workable justice.

And then, there were passengers. Their accommodation on board was segregated with their spaces out of bounds except for seniors, of whom I was now one. In their dining saloon, the Captain, Chief Engineer, and I took our meals with them. These people, harmless and nice when ashore, aboard a small ship were sometimes fractious and difficult. We, as company servants, were duty bound to please them, but I, as a new Master Mariner felt no compulsion to bow and scrape. Some sort of compromise was struck in the dining room, where simple civility dictated good manners. But I drew the line at the Scottish lady who insisted that I should stand up in the middle of my dinner.

It happened to be Hogmanay, and someone had dug up a set of bagpipes and a man who could extract the correct noises from them. At the entry of the haggis, he marched around the dining table.

'Get up! Get up!' she said sharply, her eagle eye having settled upon me, 'do ye not stand up when you hear the skirl o' the pipes?'

She was outshone by the marmalade heiress. This glamorous lady, accompanying her husband, a silver haired diplomat in the government service, was disembarking at Cyprus. She was an heiress to one of the jam making families in Bristol. Most women dressed smartly for dinner, and the marmalade heiress succeeded to a degree, but came down with her face smothered in thick lumps of a shiny grease, a skin cream – for how could it be anything else? The effect was to turn everybody's face away in silent embarrassment. She sat on the Captain's right. This was no accident, for Captain Jack had pre-selected her. The practise was to browse through the passport pictures, in advance of their bearers' arrival. The passports had been deposited as, or slightly before they boarded, with the purser/ chief steward. After shuffling through them all, Jack decided rhe seating arrangements, based on the most glamorous and fascinating, and scaled them downwards towards my seat, at the bottom of the twelve-seater table. He got the M.H., and was sorely sorry for it. She made her entrance each night, haughtily addressing her 'good evenings' to no one in particular, and glossily gooped up with the sticky substance, until, unannounced, the Admiral in charge at Limassol sent out a small frigate which stopped us in the open sea, and took off the lady and her influential husband in his pinnace.

A tall American we remembered as the lady with some spit. We had followed our regular route past Istanbul, where, prior to entering unfriendly Black Sea waters we made our usual stop off the Golden Horn to land our wartime convoy gear and codes with the British Embassy. After landing cargo at Trabzon we crossed to Bulgaria, the port of Bourgas, then staunchly red and strongly anti-West. We were to load attar of roses in drums, an unlikely cargo indeed. A column of Marxist school children appproached from a gap in the sombre concrete structures which formed the town. Our passenger watched as they paused abreast the slightly billowing ensign at our stern, and, at the timed command from their teacher, in unison, spat at it. Out on deck the lady, incensed, was working her mouth. Hanging over the rail, she spat back at the children with the greatest vigour.

Older travellers were never out of danger. A man, in his eighties, was tipped out of his steamer chair by a vicious roll, piercing his skull with a one inch bolt, and we put back to Falmouth, with his survival in the balance. And, as a group, a half dozen, at Alexandria each trip, would take the day outing to view the pyramids, eating nice green salads on the way. Always, on their return, they would seek their beds and stay there for a week, victims of 'Gyppo tummy.' We were a small group on *Pinemore* and aside from a medicine chest, the *Shipmasters Medical Guide* and the radio, were without proper medical advice.

These daily alarms any new Chief Officer can do without. I consoled myself with a practical observation. An advantage in having passengers was that we carried an extra pastry cook. The cakes (we referred to them as 'tab-nabs') and pastries were cream-filled and fluffily melted in the mouth.

It helped, also, to learn about this time that *Pinemore* would no longer send visitors ashore at Alexandria. The hatred between Jew and Arab became more bitter by the day. The Arab countries instituted new rules for keeping the enemy, his friends, and associates out. Out of our fleet of twelve, there were now to be 'Jewish' ships, and 'Arab' ships, forever to be segregated. Our Prince Line sistership, *Palestinian Prince*, in keeping with the company practise of wearing a large shield device on its bridge front reflecting its name, now had it re-styled, and the large five-pointed Star of David quickly transubstantiated into a bunch of oranges.

In Palestine, or Israel as it was grudgingly acknowledged to be after the first ten years of its existence, it appeared to me that one half of the people was nation building aggressively. The other half, of which some retained a faded tattoo bearing their death camp numbers, cherished unrighted wrongs. While at anchor off Tel Aviv, one of my sailors painted over the side on a stage. He idly doodled in the usual manner. With his round brush dripping red lead, he tried graffiti, then daubed a naked lady, a one-eyed seagull, then a *swastika*! This was spotted by dockers who rode a barge drifting out from the land. They shouted angrily and brandished their fists. But it went further. Under report, the young sailor was escorted ashore at Tel Aviv, to the jailhouse. I had to fetch him from the court, after he had paid a fine of twenty pounds.

On the farms and the kibbutzes, the citrus fruit was ready about Christmas. The faster ships overflowed the harbour at Haifa, and anchored outside, all ready to load and race back to European markets, so that they could return for another cargo, and maybe a third, before the plantations were picked bare. The Citrus Marketing Board was an efficient go-ahead body who employed all of our ships for this lucrative trade. They laid down strict rules for carriage, and ventilation of the cargo. On *Pinemore* we were specially fitted with fans in each hold, powerful enough to blast the required number of natural air changes (refrigeration was considered unnecessary for a 12 day voyage back in temperate conditions.) The loading gangs worked impressively, completing in two days. In place of the 'bruce' boxes made of slatted wood, the oranges, great juicy '*shamoutis*', were packed in cartons of 'fibrite', a strong layered cardboard. This was a new idea, the British grocery giants appeared to want it. The C.M.B. instructions were explicit. Ventilation is applied according to the temperature and dewpoint of the ambient air. The new air is pushed in, and warm damp air extracted. But the innovators ignored a scientific certainty. Warm moist air from the fruit, sodden with carbon dioxide will, when coming into contact with cold dry air from outside, condense into a corrosive acid. We experienced a sharp cooling when entering the Western approaches to the English Channel in January, and stopped all fans. The lower half of the cargo became soaked, rotting the cartons, and all that remained were tons of over-ripened oranges, pulped to flatness. The subsequent investigation revealed that we had acted correctly, as the log book of temperatures proved. The temperature drop was too much for the fans, whether run forward, reversed, or stopped. It was an act of God, and I truly thanked him for getting me off the hook.

Meanwhile, a wedding was being arranged. During the summer, we carried less inward cargo so that the time between voyages, our home leave time, was shortened. The Company kindly granted my request for a 'trip off.' But which trip to take? Judy's idea was to make a 'Gretna Green' style dash, but I stodgily moved for the full works, in church. We gambled on a date in the autumn, (spring was then approaching.) We estimated that date to lie in the middle of a voyage. In other words, it gave us plenty of leeway.

That date was approaching fast, and while I sailed the Mediterranean, those at home made dresses, chose bridesmaids, and arranged the reception, to be held, needless to say, at the New Inn, in Gloucester. I waited anxiously for news of the homeward fixture. We were no wiser when it came, as no one had heard of the place. We were ordered to Serifos. Many small islands dotted about the Greek Aegean, white arid rocks through which we threaded our way to the ports of the region. We were booked to load a full cargo of phosphate rock and Serifos turned out to be one of these, an island largely composed of the stuff. But Serifos! So small an island, so small a bay to enter, turn and lie in, so small a loading arm at the end of a fairy-sized bucket chain. Off the bay, and a place named Port Livadhi, we stopped and drifted. The local fisherman who acted as pilot, tucked in his tartan shirt, clambered out of his boat, and up to the bridge, extending a large brown hand of rawhide all around. He looked fore and aft, and side to side, with dismay written in his lined, leathery face. He had not expected a ship quite so big.

'Not possible to enter, Captain, too much wind. No, not possible.' And he climbed back down again. He knew, we all knew, that the hot dry North Easterly which blows down the Aegean, blows all summer.

Captain Jack could do no more, and so we patrolled outside. Up and down. Up and down, waiting for the wind to drop. This caused the first of the wedding day's cancellations, which I passed to Sparks to send away home.

When we did enter, everything was too small. The loading arm had not the outreach. One side of the ship was loaded first, then we turned around, before loading the other side. The process took far longer, causing the second wedding day cancellation. The distaff side threw up their hands at this stage. The day would go ahead, they said, when I arrived.

It all ended happily, for I led my Judy Gray down the aisle in September. My life changed then. This was the uneasy fate of so many seafarers. It was our separations which mattered, and how could I best mitigate them, by mixing the sea, and married life? This became all-important, the urge to advance myself and get my own ship was still there, but so was the urge to forge a new domestic life with wife, and, for sure, a family.

I returned to *Pinemore*. Captain Jack was in hot water. Jack Fergus was a slice of good fortune, for me. A warm, explosive Irishman from Lisburn, he had helped me to land more softly into my new area of responsibilty, offering guidance with good humour. But Jack, like so many, was over fond of his gin. He had had a trying voyage where he had reckoned his passengers among the undesirables, and let them know it. One of these with a mighty power in shipping circles had shopped poor Jack. A Lloyds underwriter, no less, travelling on board with his wife, had taken note of occasions when Jack was performing where he ought not to have been, in his cups.

In the marble halls of Leadenhall Street, they wanted an answer. I was called, by telegram, to the office, while at home. They took me into the Directors' room, heavy with oak desk and wine coloured carpet.

'Mr.Jones,' the M.D.said, silkily, sitting comfortably in black jacket and pin-stripes, 'we know this is a difficult question for you to have to answer. But have you ever – how shall I put it – seen Captain Fergus under the influence of too much alcohol?'

'No, Sir, never,' I lied. The tall Marine Superintendent led me back downstairs.

– A Slight Disruption –

'Well,' he pronounced, 'I must say, you were most loyal, Jones.' A pause. 'But there's no smoke without fire, of course, we know that.'

'No, sir,' I said, 'there's no smoke without fire.'

A big change came to our trading pattern. Through the American and Canadian Great Lakes, a seaway had been created. Deep sea ships, they called us 'salties', were now able to traverse the lakes as far as Duluth, at the far end of Superior, or Chicago on Lake Michigan. On *Pinemore* we were to pioneer the route through to the Windy City. They had fitted her with a stern anchor and chain, approved fairleads, new navigation lights, and landing booms. These last were for landing men to take our ropes at berths too remote for linesmen. I was lucky enough to have two young ordinary seamen who enjoyed making this dangerous leap onto a three-inch rope and descending into the darkness.

Our natural enemies were the 'Lakers', inland vessels that had worked through the old Lachine and Welland canals. It did not please them to see the upper St.Lawrence made passable. Three sets of large locks, bigger and better than those at Panama, connected the sea with Lake Ontario. The Welland Canal has eight more to lift us the height of Niagara Falls from that lake to the level of all the others.

The St. Lawrence seaway was seized upon, by shipowners, as a bounty, a munificent fillip to maritime trade. Furness Withy, with their strong shipping connections in Canada saw the possibilities of spreading all over the Eastern States, even into the mid-west. On the other hand, the railroad managers resisted strongly. They faced the prospect of seeing their traditional freight slipping through their fingers, and old ports such as New York, Philadelphia and Baltimore being bypassed. So the scene was set, but, it seemed, there was no time for rehearsals.

Aboard the ships there was some local difficulty in communications. We 'salties' had trouble with the fresh water guys, their lack of proper shipboard procedure, the Southern state drawl-speak of the muddy still-water canals. They looked askance at us, with our plummy Brit. accents, our sharp bows and steep sides so unsuited to the waterways, our diminutive rudders making our steering so skittish. Their radio phones would not correspond with ours. The mobile phone was still a pipe dream. Even walkie-talkies were too few and delicate to be of any use. To compensate, the company had fitted us with a huge short wave transmitter which hung in the wheelhouse like a kitchen cupboard. The only one who understood it was the Sparks, and he had to be turned out in plenty of time. We were approaching a narrowing of the channel near Detroit, with a Laker coming towards us in the opposite direction. We would arrive at the two channel-width markers at the same time. Sparks was sent for.

'Call 'em up, Sparkie. Tell 'em to let us come through.' The request came from our pilot, an inexperienced salt-water man.

Sea Like A Mirror

The Laker skipper's radio gave a crackle. Why did all American skippers speak with the deep, deep tones of the Mississippi watermen?

'There's enough room between them buttons for the both of us, we're comin' on down,' he declared, in a monotone. But he had a rudder twice the size of ours. There were many ship collisions and groundings, that season.

In Calumet City, cargo destined for Chicago was landed. The forbidding industrial wasteland there had turned Lake Michigan a ditchwater black. We were the first to bring a general cargo into the port, from foreign. The stevedores were unaccustomed and overloaded our gear, bending one of our tubular steel derricks to banana shape. In that opening season, *Pinemore* was one of the first ships of the type to venture as far as Chicago. This had attracted a television company, and for the run through from Montreal, we were accompanied by a film crew, with a ton or so of equipment. They recorded every important incident, sometimes going out before us in the very early morning, to film from a bridge under which we were due to pass, or record our progress through a lock. We all had our little scenes, acting for the television company, and after we had docked, were taken to the studio on the 'Loop' in downtown Chicago, and kindly given a preview, followed by cocktails, in the American manner.

Our first trip was not a success, in the matter of cargo revenues. We sailed out nearly empty, on what may have been labelled a 'loss leader' voyage, returning home only a little heavier, with bags of soy beans, and lard, loaded liquified, into one of our converted fuel oil tanks. We made one more voyage, with our sistership *Beechmore*, then were switched back into the Mediterranean. This was due to the onset of winter ice, and must have been, in some way, fortuitous, as we were not sent there again. In any case, the Atlantic trade was becoming containerised making the inland seaway intrinsically unsuitable for liner-type sailings. But the seaway has developed its potential as a direct connection between the mid-west and Europe for moving medium sized bulk cargoes, such as grain, coal, minerals and steel products.

Returning frequently to London, we were able to invite our wives for brief ship visits. Jack Fergus might bring his, and I certainly would fetch mine. These visits usually yielded a trip over to Antwerp and back. Betty Fergus was quite different from Jack. A charming lady, she and Judy Gray hit it off well. They complemented each other, Betty, silent and quietly dressed, Judy, colourful and fun loving. We made a foursome and rode up to town from the docks in a public service bus. Jack and I had indulged in the mandatory liquid refreshment, arming ourselves for the evening. Despite the signs all around the bus warning us, starkly, that *roken verboten*, we lit up our cigarettes. In Belgium, the law had no importance, for the likes of us. The bus driver, a reasonable man, stopped the bus and turned round.

'Please, no smoking aboard the bus,' he said, in perfect English. We stamped on the lighted stubs. But lit up again as soon as he started off. Judy Gray and Betty were embarassed, and remonstrated. And the bus driver stopped again.

'I'll have to ask you to get off the bus,' he said, 'I won't start off again until you do.' The girls walked off, a safe distance ahead. It was some time before they would speak to us. We were younger, then. Judy and I romped and skylarked about in the cabin, falling over the chairs. Then we knew how dangerous this was. Judy was growing big with our first child.

Chapter Nine

THE SHIP IS YOUR HOME

A sailor's place, when his wife is *enceinte,* is at home, with her. I made this observation to the gentleman standing at my cabin door.

'The ship is your home, Mr. Jones,' rumbled the Marine Superintendent.

The 'Super', Head Office's cheerless emissary, came down every day when the ship was lying in London. Even captains were awed by this figure, who had a lordly power over them. Captain Browett, conscious of his large black Homburg, inclined his silvered head at the door from fear of displacing it.

'This is your home,' he said.

They would stick with tradition, it helped them in their work. The ship had first claim on its crew. This principle had been dangled before all officers since the first square-rigged Cape Horners put to sea, and Captain Browett would never call it into question. The old dictates were, of course, a confidence trick, a bubble in the uncertain world of our boss's authority. This had been the way of things since my training ship days, the motto would still be there, I was sure of it, painted in a scroll over the games room door,

'The game is worth more than the player of the game, and the ship is worth more than the crew' and Rudyard Kipling said that, so it must be true. It would have taken a Tolpuddle martyr to deny it.

I was no martyr. I was a straightlaced company man, keeping my nose clean for that distant promotion. But the super's edict was so pretentious, I knew that I had right on my side, and so was not deterred. We had an Officers' Association which was growing in strength, and a system of leave where a man could bank his days in a credit and debit account. I had a fair amount saved. I made a more positive request, by writing to the management, stating that they must relieve me when my wife's confinement became due. I would return to whichever ship they might send me. The 'trip off' arrangement employed for our marriage, having failed the first time, was never contemplated.

The company complied, there were no arguments.

Neither should there have been. The event, even Captain Browett would have conceded, was the happy replay of an all-time miracle. It had timed itself nicely with the ship's arrival, and happened at home, in the bedroom. I stood with the midwife, clutching her current anodyne – gas and air through a smelly rubber mask clumsily applied. Judy Gray struggled bravely through a long period of labour, and, at last the baby made her entrance. Our first daughter Jackie came skidding out like a small ship on launch, wrinkly pink and flour dusted, a redhead lustily bellowing, and weighing a respectable nine and a half pounds.

Just as prompt and inexorable, the call came to join a new ship. These calls, breaking in upon such brief periods of happy domesticity were becoming grim and dreadful. Until the moment when the telegram boy arrived with a small orange envelope, we had pushed the occasion to the back of our minds. Each extra day was lent an added value and we always hoped, blindly, for more.

But the 'get ready' letter had dropped onto the mat two weeks previously. The ship was *Madulsima*.

If ever there was a snob society of ships, *Madulsima* could claim to be one of their number. She was time chartered to the most 'pukka' of companies, Thos.and Jno. Brocklebank of Liverpool, long established on the run to Red Sea ports, Ceylon, Madras and Calcutta. Brocklebank's own ships were built with too many small holds full of odd spaces, nooks and crannies. *Madulsima* possessed spacious, uncluttered holds, flush decks for fork lift operation, and four huge deep-tanks for liquids. A Furness owned vessel, with the original name of *Rowanmore*, her cabin furniture was all of primrose yellow plastic, but she was ideally suited for large and difficult pieces of cargo.

From her berth in the Royal Docks, she sailed with a general cargo which included a tank landing craft, piggyback, across the deck, and a 'Jones' mobile crane below. The LCT was cared for by two RAF personnel, who were to live on board, until the craft reached its final destination at Gan, in the Maldives, an atoll with a military airstrip.

Before that, however, the Jones crane was to be landed at Mukalla, an anchorage port in the Hadramaut Yemen. And to accomplish this, the RAF were persuaded to loan out their craft. This was to be put in the water by our own fifty-ton jumbo derrick, and the crane then put into it. The craft was to be run up the pebbly foreshore. The townspeople would then come down with ropes, and haul the crane up the beach, and into the town. These tasks were all carried out successfully. *Madulsima* was good at that sort of thing. That is why Brocklebanks liked her so much. At Calcutta, they filled her up with bales of jute and chests of tea, and sent her home.

Next voyage, she did not do so well, and they changed their minds. It was 'Spunky' Duncan and the tube expander that were the cause of the trouble. Marine engineers were at that time hard to come by. The junior men of the department were numerous enough, many had come to sea to avoid compulsory military service. But the seniors, men of some value, were in demand ashore, in the shipyards and machine shops. Some of the 'Chiefs' were below calibre. Duncan, a heavy brash man from Glasgow, had held down the 'Chief's' job on a variety of ships, but not for long. *Madulsima* was equipped with a modern motor, a seven cylinder Burmeinster Wein. This main engine relied on auxiliaries powered by steam. The provider of the steam was a small 'thimble tube' boiler. Thimbles took the place of tubes. A design fault caused the boilers to burn out the tips of their tubes more often than they should. A plentiful supply of spare tubes was carried, to effect repairs on board. They were inserted with a tool, a tube expander.

Having cleared the Red Sea, we were rolling our way down, in a moderate southwesterly monsoon, towards Colombo in Ceylon. A call from the engine room went up to the bridge.

'It's only a wee problem. We have to stop.'

The boiler had fizzled out. No steam for the pumps meant that the engine must be stopped. 'Spunky' Duncan had sent his Second down, everything would be alright in a couple of minutes. Captain Kilburn was worried. He had concern for the ship, but was doubly anxious, for he knew that he should have got rid of Duncan, long ago. Only the kindness of his nature had prevented it. The boiler needed new tubes, but nobody could find the tube expander. Nobody ever found the tube expander. The airwaves between the bridge radio shack and the technical department in Leadenhall Street grew ever more frantic.

We were totally without power, and hoisted two oil burning red not-Under-Command lights to the yardarm. Even the fresh water dried up, the tank manhole was removed and water carried aft, in buckets. For five days, she rolled all the more heavily, lying in the trough of a lumpy swell, as lifeless as a dead whale.

*Our rescuer, **Smit** tug Elbe, later named **Greenpeace**.*

A Dutch salvage tug was steaming back, not far from our position, on her way to Rotterdam. She had taken a tow out East, but in the way of the salvage business, listened out, day and night, for distresses, with highly sophisticated radio. She sent over a friendly message,

'I am aware of your problems. Could we be of any assistance?'

Poor Captain Kilburn! Should he say 'yes' and sign the Lloyds Open Form of no cure – no pay, with massive cost to our insurers? Or leave us to wallow there in hopes of finding the tube expander?

'What do *you* think we should do?' He asked me up to his cabin.

'What do London say?' I said.

London, despairingly, replied

'If you've done all you can, take the tow.'

The Schmit tug *Elbe* had been lying stopped, with her predatory hull down just below the horizon. In an instant she came up and over, put on board the end of a great coir and chain tow rope which I, with my anchor party, attached to our anchor chain. We commenced a six day tow to Colombo.

We all suffered for 'Spunky' Duncan's ineptitude. When we returned to London, a wave of displeasure greeted us. Brocklebanks had angrily terminated the charter, saying that we were unfitted for their service. We reverted, like Cinderella at the stroke of midnight, to our old trampship livery, and the name of *Rowanmore*. Her future was now uncertain, and the company held us on board despite the leave we were due. Jobless, the ship was sent away.

Just below King Harry's ferry, in Cornwall, lining the right bank of the River Fal, there is a chain of ships temporarily unemployed. They form a disconsolate column, moored with their anchor cables, stem to stern for most of the reach, with reddened paintwork running rust, waiting silently for jobs. We joined the line, and Captain Browett came aboard to shut us down. The chandler put on board a supply of paraffin heaters, a portable oven, and six pump-up Aladdin pressure lamps.

'Be careful, now, with those gas mantles,' Browett said, 'they'll break just looking at 'em.'

He provided a small boat, with an outboard motor, for food shopping. We learned to navigate the river in the cold dark nights, making visits to the pub, at Malpas. Home leave was now overdue, and we demanded it. It seemed to me that, while at Falmouth, we had served our period of penance. With difficulty, they dug up reliefs (there were only three of us) and, having passed on our experiences of living without luxuries, we left her, never looking back.

New fathers coming home from sea enter new areas of conflict. Babies, brought unsuitable gifts by rumbustious strangers unused to offering their love, take refuge in their mother's arms. These self-same arms are those demanded by father, and mother will have a troubled time dispensing their favours. Judy Gray never did, and she and I carried on as before the days of children, all the while listening and looking, after the first two lightning weeks, for the orange envelope. On *Rowanmore* this came soon, and surprised us so completely that we sat, sofa bound and speechless for half a day, and Judy Gray cried most piteous tears. They had found employment for *Rowanmore* much more quickly than anyone had hoped for. She was time chartered to another tramp company, and, to my consternation, the one most likely to keep me from home for nine months or more.

'It could be less,' I told her.

'What use was that?' she said.

I climbed aboard the train back to Falmouth with a heavy heart. As we rushed through the English countryside, leaving behind everything that meant so much to me, I saw my own peace disappearing, the way to live a proper life was slipping through my fingers. I made up my mind. At King Harry there was a pay-phone. I called the management, in London. No. I was sorry, but I could not accept this appointment. Please send someone else, I would wait here until they came. Captain Browett came.

'Mr.Jones. We don't like being played ducks and drakes with,' adding in suitable shades of mournful/severe, 'we're sending down Mr.Smith to relieve you.'

*Little Ben had been made Captain of Cyprian Prince
(reproduced by kind permission of the Furness Group archives).*

This interview left a deep impression. I felt stripped of my stripes, and, worse than that, I felt guilty.

Small ships – because they would ensure short trips – that is what I wanted, and I let them know. Prince Line operated four of these little ones in their Med. fleet. Built small they fitted handily into small places. There was the *Cyprian* and *Maltese*, the *Norman* and *Northumbrian,* all of them popular ships. I had been quick to note that my friend of *Oakmore* days, Ben Londis, had been promoted captain of the *Cyprian*. Another reason why small ships, perhaps, gave a lead that I should follow! They offered me the mate's job, on the *Norman Prince*.

Norman Prince possessed only three holds but still found room for the customary twelve passengers. She took her cargoes to and from Manchester, without visiting London, and was an 'Arab' ship – after Malta and Cyprus she called at Alexandria, Beirut, and Lattakia, missing out Israel altogether.

The Manchester Ship Canal was a waterway of such evil blackness, any seaman would tell you that, should you ever fall in, then straight up to the hospital with you, and quickly to the stomach pump department. It looked that way to me, as I turned off the Trafford Road, and onto No.7 Dock, Salford. These grubby acres lay in a landlocked corner, so far inland that any connection with the sea appeared most unlikely. I should have given its worthy Victorian engineers a little more credit. The passage of thirty-five miles was long and slow, but adequately deep, with four well engineered and sizable locks to change levels. The barren banks in between were scarred and blackened by the industrial waste the gentlemen left behind, but found their way in the end, winding through Warrington to Runcorn where they followed the line of the Mersey river. *Norman Prince*, her livery pearl grey and white, with red-black funnel bearing the feathered *fleur de lys* showed as a startling splash of colour in that industrial gloom. After a long day's steaming, (or two or three when fog closed the canal down and we laid by at Latchford) we might reach the Mersey, and at last, the cleansing sea. After one voyage, I became accustomed to the routine. The seaport of Manchester was no different from London, Liverpool, Hull or Glasgow. And happily, it brought me home at frequent intervals. Also, my family could visit me. This happened one Christmas. We were to lie in Liverpool with our inbound cargo until after the holidays. I sent for my wife and baby daughter, they could stay on board with me, in a passenger cabin. Everything was arranged. She caught the morning train to Lime Street Liverpool.

By the time she reached there, we had gone, with our orders changed. We had, many times, rehearsed the procedures for such an event. She would phone the local Agent, company office, etc., but the experience was unnerving, in the extreme, for both of us, particularly as she had our babe in her arms. There were no means of contact while she was *en train*. Only the Dock Gate policeman could help, and he was the one who told her that we had gone, shifted up to Manchester, to save a little down-time. A Liverpool cabbie turned out to be the hero in this little drama.

'I've been to sea myself, love,' he said, 'I'll look after you and we'll find that ship together, sure.' He turned his cab around and headed through the Mersey tunnel for Eastham, the first lock of the canal.

'Norman Prince ?' the lockmaster said, 'she went through an hour ago!'

The same at Runcorn. At Latchford, the lock was levelling. The ship was rising at a nice steady rate. A taxi rushed up, braking at the first bollard. As the bulwark rail rose up to dock level, two of my sailors, one on each arm lifted my wife over. Our good Chief Steward, Charlie Massey, a veteran of the old school, took charge of the baby. He showed my two girls to their stateroom, with tea on a silver service, as I let go the bow-rope.

Eleven voyages bound me to the *Norman*. I was proud of her, she was as spruce as a little yacht when I left. The sailors were, no doubt, pleased to see me go, there were not many chief mates who had them out holy-stoning the wooden decks at seven each morning.

– THE SHIP IS YOUR HOME –

Our second child was on her way. Sarah, the skinny ash-blonde with the near-invisible cowlick was born, but not until I had arrived home to give some cheer and support. It was another 'planned launch'. I passed from ship to ship. I relieved other men, for their leave, staying close for the post-natal days. I looked quite seriously, now, for a position ashore, but there was nothing which would pay my disproportionate mortgage, apart from becoming a marine pilot, and Trinity House was flooded with applicants, more qualified than I. I wanted to be at home, with my wife. At the same time the mode of living at sea had taken a hold. They said that I had 'the sea in my blood.' I wanted out, there were good enough jobs to be had for an ambitious man. And yet, and yet? I hesitated. With mute understanding, Mr.Collins, our new manager in personnel, found me something new.

The *Bardic* was another ship seeking employment. She had been one of Prince Line's, named *Cingalese Prince*, and chartered to Shaw Savill, but they now had better and faster freeze ships for their New Zealand lamb and butter trade, and *Bardic* became redundant.

Far away on a Pacific atoll, General de Gaulle was building a nuclear test site for his first bomb. The French company Messageries Maritimes had been engaged to transport all manner of construction equipment, and two thousand tons of bagged cement. M.M., in turn, chartered the *Bardic* for the round voyage. We loaded at Le Havre for Papeete, in Tahiti, the closest point to its final destination We also took on M. Bouchier, a supercargo, with his supply of *vin de table*, a 'tween deck locker full, sufficient for the voyage.

Captain Browett crossed to France to have a last look round. The ship had been in drydock, and we were straightening up the mess, making her shipshape. The 'Super' had authorised an area of ships' side plating to be sand blasted clear of rust and paint. Browettt was limited, by scarcity of funds, to the 'wind and water' strakes only. This had left the top strake, the 'sheer,' in a ragged unchipped affront to the eye. My sailors were all newly signed up, their funds were low, and they were asking for overtime work. Captain Browett walked on board on that very Sunday, when all ten of them were over the side on stages, chipping and scaling industriously, cleaning off the sheer strake.

'Well done, well done, Mr.Jones!' said the 'Super', 'that's just the ticket. Keep up the good work.' It took away some of the sourness of our last meeting.

The South Pacific around Polynesia was so near to paradise that any rational person might have demanded to know why any power should want an atom bomb exploded here or anywhere else. But they were all at it, the British at Christmas Island, the Americans at Bikini and Eniwetok. France chose Mururoa, about a day's run south-east of the island. We found Tahiti, a dot in a great expanse of ocean, without a search, shaping up the last few miles on the strength of my sextant star observations in the morning. A sloping sided volcano shape, she had a halo of white woolly cloud. There was a ring of coral around her, and all ships entered through a pass, marked by buoys. As we drew near, the sweetest scents drifted out, loaded onto the balmy air, perfumes from the island's flora, bougainvillaea, gardenias, perhaps. Frangipani, certainly. None of us with a botanist's comprehension, we nevertheless breathed in the welcome fragrances greedily. This was an exceptional pleasure after many weeks of the ocean's unexceptional airs. When we reached our berth it was followed by another, the circling around us of her comely people. Large, well covered, with high gloss jet-black tresses and skins of teakwood brown, they came with infectious laughing, smiling, and showing the whitest teeth. Many among them clung to traditional dress, covering their bodies with the briefest of sarongs, both men and women, happy and relaxed with their shapes, which were, though generous, smooth skinned and beautiful. How different were they from the people at our next stop, in Melanesia. With a small quantity of cargo for Noumea, in New Caledonia, we found the stature and general mien of the people, after Tahiti, caused some disillusionment.

Back with our own white kind, we touched the Australian coast at Brisbane, with bulk phosphates loaded long ago in Hamburg when M.Bouchier first joined. We completed at Cairns, and attempted to sail in a gale that blew fiercely on-shore. The berth at which we lay was broadside onto the wind, and I was told to run a long rope up the dock, a warping line to pull her off by. It was the best seven-inch sisal I had, out of a half dozen up there on the fo'c'sle. It twanged a lot, dripping water, and finally parted with a rifle shot crack that rang out across the harbour, and we drifted down, with the prospects of a damaging crash landing.

'Get another one out! Send off another!'

From the bridge, came the cry. A good sailor's throwing arm, expert with the heaving line was called for. Happily, we had one. Able Seaman Goodwin saved the day.

'Oh, well done, sailor! Well done,' the cry again came down.

Repeats of this incident were bound to happen. I had another grand idea. At Townsville, I sat down and wrote a letter to the Port Commissioners at Cairns. At a British shipyard, (I wrote) I would build a tugboat (the port had none) sail it out to their port, and supply towage services to the Port of Cairns. I would finance the deal with money from their approved bank, in Queensland. The reply was brief, but polite. They rarely had the need of boats, but, when they did, they would order one up from Brisbane, thank you very much.

The homeward leg had commenced. We took on a steamy hot consignment of metal concentrates at Townsville, for Le Havre, which seemed an impressive distance away. The weight of this would act as ballast, as our main homeward cargo consisted of the flesh of the coconut – copra. The cargo lay waiting at various small points around the New Hebrides, commencing with Port Vila. Here we tied up alongside a white administrative building which flew the French flag and the British, side by side. This was a dual administration held by the two countries jointly. Since the Napoleonic wars control of this small island group had been in contention, and what we saw before us represented a sunny compromise. We did learn, however, that headhunting tribes were not completely eliminated from the islands. As we strolled back, at night, from the small hut, thatched with leaves, where we were able to buy cold Australian beer, we held very much to the centre of the rough track between dark trees leading back to the ship.

The copra came aboard loose, in bulk, as clean white pieces the size of orange peelings. It had been dried in the sun, and would be ready, after its long voyage, for its soap-making oil to be extracted. It was loaded from lighters, eventually filling all five holds, the solid stow vertically pierced by ventilator shafts, constructed by the loading gangs from chicken wire wrapped around a wooden frame.

We began the long haul, through the Torres Strait and Suez, back to France.

The sun was very high in the sky at that time of the year. Christmas had passed without any to-do, almost unnoticed in the switching between islands, and we did little to celebrate but drink the canned beer and stodgily munch the requisite fare. *Bardic*, in the sun, became an oven, with the copra slowly cooking down below. In the Arafura Sea there was no wind, no relief from wet humidity. The ship was without air conditioning, so that sleeping and eating, instead of a comfort, became chores to put up with.

At our table in the saloon, there sat five. Captain and Mrs. Williams with myself, the Chief, and M. Bouchier. Mrs. Williams, until then, had put up a brave show. Captain Williams had tried his very best to ginger up light dinner time conversation, ever since leaving Le Havre, but he was no master at this, and M. Bouchier was most economical with his English. The Chief was a shy man, new to the job and more diffident than he needed to be. I was too stuffily taken up with my affairs in the running of the deck to concern myself. Mealtimes, as the voyage progressed, became more and more silent. Any attempt to give an old story a fillip provoked nothing but a toe-curling discomfort. And that was before the invasion.

We were seated around a limp white table-cloth, waiting for our soup, and perspiring gently under our constricting cotton clothes. Mrs. Williams gave a squeak, a sort of suppressed scream. A glossy black insect, smaller than a ladybird sallied out across the cloth. Yet another appeared glued into the melting butter dish. She had squealed at receiving her first bite, the first of many. The beetles had just found their way out of the cargo spaces, whole armies of them, battalions of 'copra bugs'. One might have been able to bear them, if they had not bitten. But they attacked ever more viciously, at table, in the bathroom, and in bed, foraying upon the most intimate parts. This onslaught continued as long as the tropic temperatures persisted. The suppressed screams of poor Mrs. Williams, with occasional flaps at the butter dish with her napkin, competed for the silence, with the rattle of the ceiling (or deckhead) fans, all the way to Suez.

Half the copra went off at Marseilles. We steamed around to Le Havre to complete, and M.Bouchier went home. There remained a quantity of his wine and he divided it up between us. Also, generous 'envelopes' came aboard from Messageries, for Captain Williams, and me. *Bardic* found herself unemployed again, and Furness Withy sold her to the Bibby Line. The Furness fleet was dwindling away, and the first signs of an industry suffering a sea-change started to appear. An American firm called Sealand, which had been shipping goods up to Alaska pre-packed in large boxes so as to reduce the amount of handling, had standardised the size of its box. It measured, in feet, twenty by eight by eight, and they christened it, suitably enough, a 'container'.

Personnel put me on the *Pinemore* again. Nothing had changed aboard her, but she was a little run down, a good tidy up and a fresh coat of paint was needed. It came as no surprise when Captain Browett came down on a regular visit. He was even grumpier than usual.

'I want this ship cleaned up, Mr. Jones! Look at this! And this! And this!'

I followed him around in the practiced way, noting the unpolished brass door strips, the teak brightwork long unwashed, the running wires, innumerable wires lying uncoiled upon the open deck, a constant danger.

'Last week I was on the *Beechmore* and she was a sight smarter than this,' he said. Browett often employed this ruse of comparing a sistership more favourably. I was fortunate in having a good Bosun (though he was soon to be dismissed, when apprehended by the dock gate policeman with three new paint-brushes he had 'borrowed' to do up his home) and between us we worked to make Captain Browett, and our better selves, happier. She had her name changed to *African Prince* to spice up the trade, and her colours from black, to grey. She now became the smartest of all the Med. ships, in my eyes, at least. Even Browett was satisfied. I had a friend in Captain Ken Slapp, we saw things in the same way, and he encouraged me to apply for a 'Pacific' boat, putting in a good word. These were the top-flight ships, senior Chief Officers laid claim to them, and guarded the jobs, jealously. They ran only out to the West Coast of the U.S.A., and Vancouver in British Columbia, the same route I had followed in the *Welsh Prince* fourteen years before. The trips were short, about three months, and regular.

On board *Pacific Envoy* the same cargoes of whisky littered the ocean floor in our wake with pilfered bottles, recovered and dumped. It was all on shrink-wrapped pallets, now. At a recent drydocking, the holds had been squared off by building floor to ceiling bulkheads, suitable for palletised cargo, handled by fork-lift. Competition with the new container ships, run by the Swedes, was fierce. But there was a warm company spirit alive on the coast. From Long Beach, northwards, each port helped the next towards a successful turn-round. I made many American friends, in the agencies and stevedore companies, and some English ones too, very often it was hard to distinguish between the two. The California sunshine was hard to beat, and a few dollars would buy you luxury.

My future promotion to captain, was looking more and more unattainable. I had to do something. Every shipping company was trimming its fleets. The new container ships being built in Japan and Korea were taking over traditional trades. These ships were, for sure, the ships of the future, despite some die-hard owners' cries to the contrary. Each of them would displace five or six of my kind, with, it had to be realised, five or six captain's jobs. They even made inroads into our very own whisky trade, no-one could steal from those sealed, iron-bound boxes. And lastly, but not leastly, there were the heart breaking farewells each time my wife and family, and I, were separated. My third daughter had arrived. Becky came when I was at sea. She confounded the medics by arriving a few weeks early, on my last *Pinemore* voyage, and her head was wetted, on board, a splendid ceremony her sisters could never match.

Out on the West Coast, friends and helpers fell over themselves. Mike Brown, a cargo superintendent in Portland, Oregon came close to making a stevedore out of me, and up in Vancouver, Stan Woolgar, our regular supercargo, put down my name as a candidate for admission into his very select closed shop. But this was not now. I had to have something I could step right into, we could not live on fresh air. About that time, Elmer, from Vancouver Tug and Barge visited me on board. We used his small tugs when berthing at the Canadian Pacific dock.

'Why don't you come on out here?' he suggested. His promise was an echo of so many others.

'We'll fix you up on one of our boats,' he said, 'towing log rafts around the Sound. Something better will come along.'

To enter Canada was easy, there was even to be had an assisted passage for genuine immigrants. All the signs pointed this way. While in Vancouver, on my fourth *Envoy* voyage, I addressed my letter to the Personnel Department in London.

I wished to leave, I said. The future was not bright, there was not much hope of promotion in the conditions then prevailing. I would find shore employment in Canada, in keeping with my qualifications. And, would they, please, undertake to transport my effects (just a small quantity), together with my two spaniels, out to Vancouver, without charge?

I would go out quietly, without fuss. My last voyage ended in Manchester. The *Pacific Envoy* was built to fit tightly the locks throughout the waterway, between each side and the lock wall there was just enough space for a wooden fender. And, at each, to make room, we must let go the stern tug, and pick it up on the other side. Height was also a factor. To allow passage under a number of bridges, at Eastham there was a layby for vessels to lower topmasts, and remove high smoke stacks. Our telescopic topmast, though, lowered helpfully into a tabernacle formed by the hollow mainmast. To lower completely, all attachments to the mast must be cleared of obstructing fittings. It was my responsibility. Regrettably, the hounds-bands were not slackened, they were left in place by uninformed sailors, three feet of the mast still protruded.

The railway bridge at Runcorn took the strain. First the trip-wire parted, strumming, on contact with our topmast lightning conductor. Then the mast hit the bridge, and with a rending screeching sound bent at an angle which allowed us to pass underneath.

I would not go out so quietly, now. I was called to a short interview in London, with Captain Browett, but no mention was made of this incident. It was warm inside, and without his homburg he seemed almost human.

'We'll help with your effects, Mr. Jones. But your dogs. Surely you can get rid of them, and buy two more when you get out there?' There *was* a hint of sympathy, I noted.

No, I could not get rid of the dogs. The kids could go first.

'Well, well. We don't like losing a good Chief Officer, you know.' He regarded his shoes. 'But I think you are doing the right thing, Jones.'

Captain Browett offered a hand, to be shaken.

Chapter Ten

AMERICAN DREAM

———

'How were they, then?' I was anxious to know, and even neglected to shake hands. 'The dogs, I mean.'

'Oh, I know quite well who you mean,' said Captain Meldrum of the *Loch Loyal*, with a rueful chuckle,

'Well. They were fine up until Cristobal, and then the bitch took a lump out of a black longshoreman who only wanted to make friends.'

I could picture it. My Gill did not take kindly to singular strangers. Better to have been her softish son, travelling beside her in a twin kennel. He was sorely missing the family, by then, and would have overturned, belly up, at any extended hand. Captain Meldrum suggested that I went below, to the cadets' quarters, where the boys had care of them. For the customary bonus, which was well deserved, they had walked the dogs, cared for, fed, and tidied up after them, night and day, while traversing two oceans and the Panama Canal. This was going to be a joyful reunion.

My two spaniels more closely resembled a pair of piglets. They waddled over towards me listlessly, looking for a tasty bite, and I was not at all sure they even remembered me. They were out of condition, and their wavy roan 'frills' had lost their springy gloss. Innocently enough, when quizzed, the younger of the two boys revealed the truth of the matter. A pair of sweet lady passengers, while passing their drawn-out sea days at the fake log fire which glowed perpetually in their panelled lounge, had pampered the animals by dispensing a bottomless tube of chocolate biscuits. This had put paid to the dogs' tolerable figures. I arranged for their boarding kennels, out in the suburb of Coquitlam. Also stowed in the hold were the most transportable of our family treasures, the old Welsh dresser, a pricey Axminster, silver table ware and china, and a few good clothes. These had been crated up, and kennels made for the dogs in time for the ship's sailing.

The *Loch Loyal*, a fast modern motorship, belonged to Royal Mail Lines, another company affiliated with Furness, and had been grouped with our 'Pacific' boats. For six long weeks before she arrived with my dogs, I had roamed the streets of Vancouver job searching, at times hard up and always hungry, and the *Loch Loyal* wilted my resolve further by handing out my first dose of homesickness. This was surely a malady to which I was, at this stage of my life, immune. But the homely flower-printed cretonnes and the fragrance of polished wood in Captain Meldrum's dayroom carried palpable reminders of an English home. That particular home, I told myself firmly, was behind me, now.

Furness had kept their word. They shipped my freight *gratis*, but the dogs were charged to my account. My friends at Empire Stevedoring came to the pier with a pick-up truck, and helped me put the packed goods into storage. The plan was to leave my family in England until I obtained employment, anything lowly would do, to start, just 'to keep the wolf from the door.' Simultaneously, my wife would handle the sale of the house, send the dogs away in care of our good friend, John White, have our boxed-up treasures deposited on board *Loch Loyal*, and wait for word from me to come, tasks which were harder for her, than the ones I had allotted myself.

The non-stop jumbo flight put me down at Vancouver International on a rainy day in February. I found a room at the Missions to Seamen, on Robson Street. One or two phone calls, I told myself, and the job offers would come flooding in. Waiting was not easy. Elmer at Vancouver Tug and Barge, was perplexed to find me, one day, descended out of the distant blue, knocking at his office door. Now, faced with the reality, he was unwilling to see me, a holder of a Master's ticket, on his boats as a casual deck hand. Dubious, he took me down to a small tug, where, as one of these, I would earn around four dollars an hour. I discovered to my discomfort that I would lay my head to sleep against a heavy piece of 8"x 4" semi-hardwood which formed the little vessel's stem bar. We chugged out under the Lions Gate bridge a little way, as far as Port Mellon, brought back an empty chip barge, and laid the boat up again. Employment was truly casual. In the winter months, men who worked for most of the year out of town in the lumber industry came down from the hills, and snapped up any vacancies. At the break of a day I would sooner forget, I was beaten by another, at the labour hiring hall, to a position as floor cleaner in the big central hotel. I found it necessary to call upon my wife to send out remittances, and pawned my watch one day, for supper, when these, due to no fault of hers, did not arrive.

My serious applications had been made for employment with B.C. coastal ferries, the two major stevedoring companies and, most desirable of all, the jealously preserved membership of the Supercargoes Association. This was the 'plum', a freelance group of men whom I had observed from ship to ship, hiring themselves out at high rates to shipowners, overseeing all aspects of the cargo work, and managing the labour. My friend Stan Woolgar, himself a supercargo and one-time London tally clerk, had entered my name on the lists. But that was sometime in the misty future, I needed something, now, more and more urgently. Every stone in the City of Vancouver had been turned. All I could do was sit as still as I was able, surrounded by the Mission's budget furniture, guarding a limp sandwich and exchanging commiserations with my two companions. One of these was a 'lifer', a Newfoundland sailor newly released from jail for having murdered his wife. The other, Colin, from Antrim, a young seafarer, like me looking to swallow the anchor, for good. Colin had just been interviewed for the position of ladies' shoe salesman, had got the job, and was starting in the shop next day.

'Anybody can do it,' he said, 'you should give it a try.'

Nothing could have darkened the day more. Never, never, never could I see myself selling shoes.

At home, Judy Gray was becoming restless. This was the day on which she should have come, the airline tickets for four were booked. But I had sent off to her to cancel, I had found nothing. We were in contact from day to day, and she had sold the house to our friends, Chris. and John. This was worse than a sea voyage, the uncertainty, the feeling of fate working and scheming to our ultimate unhappy end.

The Mission's manager walked in.

'Anyone here want the third mate's job on *Tyee Shell*? The office just called, they need a man right away,' he said, directing his look at me. I rushed down to the agency on Burrard. The *Tyee Shell* was a small coastal tanker. She loaded up in Vancouver with products for the backwater lumber towns of British Columbia, oil for the basement stoves, aviation gas for the single engined seaplanes, she carried every grade. I was accepted.

I would look for lodgings for my family right away. I must tell Judy Gray it was all on again, get the airline bookings back!

'Leaving the *country*?' the gas man had boomed down the phone. She had told him he must disconnect in less than the vital twenty-four hours.

Then, they all came. Three little girls mute and wide eyed, my lovely wife, her chestnut locks uneasy in the airport's breezes, stepped from the plane. Now, things were really happening. I had the dogs taken care of. We had stored the old Welsh dresser. Now I *really* had some caring to do. We rented a small house belonging to an Indian, in Burnaby. We charged to my account four beds, a lounge suite of sorts, and some dining room furniture. The hardest thing was to tell her, though, that I would be leaving her in a couple of days, and sailing out again.

Tyee Shell puttered out through the Second Narrows quietly and without fuss, there was no need of pilot or tugs. She was loaded full and down, her decks washing over with the green waters of Vancouver harbour. Prince Rupert, a couple of days away, was as far as she would sail with drop-off points in between, extending occasionally to Hyder, in Alaska. All coastal traffic held to the easy inland route, but the strength of the tide in full spate forced our first stop, at Seymour Narrows, where we 'made doughnuts', circling, awaiting slack water at the turn. The first cargo stop was at Bella Bella where we went alongside a short wooden jetty built on piles. The crew connected the flexible hoses, one for stove oil, the other for tractor diesel. Some distance from the ship, the storage tanks were safely sited up in the tree line, out of sight of all, in a country no-man's land.

'Now then, Alan.' The mate, a local Vancouver man who had yearned to go to sea, but gloomily admitted that Canada's merchant service could offer nothing better than this, put one quietening hand on my shoulder.

'See, your job is to dip the tanks. Take the radio, the flashlight, and that metal measuring tape with you, and the guy up at the tank farm will show you what to do.'

The guy up at the tank farm did not like to stand long in the rain that was then falling softly through the tall pines. In the damp, coal-black darkness he gave me precious few guidelines.

'Put some paste on y're tape at the full height of the tank, and call 'em down at the boat, on the radio, to stop pumping when you get a bitty two feet off the top. The paste 'll discolour. An' lookit! Have an eye through yon trees, that's whar the brown bears come down fro', rootin' roun', lookin' for stuff. They ain't vicious, so long as you treat 'em right.'

Attached to the side of the round, silver-painted tank, now slippery with rain, was a steel ladder. I climbed it to the top, and unscrewed the central plug, to be struck by a blast of rich petroleum fumes, swirling and seeking an escape from the pressure of the ship's pumps. I lowered down the tape. The paste, which I applied with my forefinger washed away down the tape, with the rain, which was, by this time dripping from the end of my nose. I could see nothing, in any case, the flashlight offered up no more than nearby object's reflections.

'Just shine your flashlight down, Alan. You'll see the level coming up. Give us a call before it gets anywhere near,' the mate responded anxiously, over the radio.

This was misery, abject and wet. The radio, happily, continued to function, and I knew when I should stop them. It was with the tank 'filled', well short of the top, which I judged by the changing note in the whistle of expelled air, and not caring a jot for the bears, I hurried back to the ship, as dry and warm a refuge to be found, anywhere in that pine forest.

The trips were short. I managed to reach home at each visit to the quay at Shellburn. Judy had found a school for the children, and the local supermarket. It was her first time out of England, she managed exttremely well. But, as she pointed out, we did not come out here, just to *manage*. 'Just think what we left,' she said.

I picked up some new trade tricks long forgotten by the big ship sailors. This was the coastal trade, as my home-grown shipmates were quick in pointing out to any deep-sea man with fancy airs. Steaming up the narrow creeks, they said, the skipper has no need of your new-fangled radar to gauge the distance from the shore. When the fog comes down, he blows the siren and counts the seconds for the echo to come back.

'It worked on the old *Princess Patricia*, and she carried a load of passengers,' they said.

A supertanker caught fire in the eastern Pacific. A deep sea tug had secured the burned out vessel, taking her in to Nootka Sound, a landlocked bay on the west coast of Vancouver island. *Tyee Shell* was chartered to lighten her. We would shuttle some of her cargo, making six trips down to an oil terminal in Tacoma, across the border in Washington State. I climbed aboard the fire-blackened wreck at Nootka Inlet. Here was a chance for somebody! The fire had only reached the upperworks, the hull and machinery were still intact. But she was an insurance case, a 'constructive total loss'. If I could purchase her, at a low price, with a loan from the bank, and refurbish her, putting my crew on board, I should quickly become a prosperous shipowner. I seriously considered the pros and cons, but my stodgy caution won, and my courage failed me. I always regretted this, as I might, just, have made it.

Some of my leads were now producing results. The Supercargoes Association advised that my name had gone onto a short list. Simultaneously, my friend Mike Brown, a stevedore manager over the border in Portland, Oregon, who had for long held his ear to the ground, came forward with grapevine news. In Seattle, he advised, States Steamship Company was looking for an 'Operations man,' and he had told them all about me. My induction into the maritime life of the Puget Sound had begun.

Harbours on the Sound, in that year of '68, were hosts to strange old grey-hulled ships newly re-emerged, as if hatched, from under their preserving 'mothballs.' The Vietnam wastage was at its height, and all the way from Port Angeles to Tacoma the grey ships were loading all manner of goods from bombs and ammunition to toothpaste and beer. Manpower of the seagoing kind was sparse, and the ships were going away with navigators as unlikely as Queequeg.

Any competent mate who had stowed things in a ship's hold had a price on his head, anyone who could sort out whether Da Nang or Saigon lots came out first, and how many longshore gangs it would take to finish off every hold at the same time. I was such a one. Being British, and until recently sailing under that nation's flag, finishing up in this place would be a normal, natural occurrence. There were many of us. A school of British seafarers, high and dry upon the shore, filled a need in the employment market and, mascot-like, decorated shipping offices from California to the Pacific Northwest. I loved the coast. I knew they needed me. And looking back, I know that they – not without the warmth of American kindness – knew that I needed them. We both knew that I could no longer leave my young family fatherless by snatches, and that this was a condition I had sought to change, for years. With time-off from my port watchkeeping on *Tyee Shell*, I proceeded with all speed down Interstate 5 to Seattle in a rented Ford, arriving at the corner of Second and Cherry where States Line leased a floor of a nineteen-twenties high-rise. It lay within a stone's throw of Seattle's Skid Row, down which the logs slithered to the water before there was ever a ship or a harbour. I took Judy Gray along with me. I had heard that in America they liked to see your wife, as well. They did, and she was, as ever, a great asset to me. The interview was so successful that they found a place for me as understudy to their Port Captain, in Vancouver, while I and my family awaited our green card immigrants' visas. This took some time. Even Senator Magnusson's office, when asked to expedite, replied with,

'We might be able to speed things up, were it not for applicants asking to be hurried through!'

The 'hurry' ended eight months later. A self-drive five ton truck was hired which we loaded up and drove, with some difficulty. With a mortgage on a rambler style house in Lake Forest Park, we moved in without delay, with the children, the dogs, and all our earthly goods.

It was not all about the war. In fact, the embattled lands of south east Asia appeared only as another destination for our cargoes. Far outnumbering the old grey C2s were Seattle's smarter ships, the sleek white fleet of the States Line. These vessels were, arguably, the finest general cargo carriers ever built. They were the ultimate ships of their kind, and the last, as the container vessel was then coming into its own and would soon displace them. Their design was the result of a progression. All shipbuilding Stateside was performed under subsidy, an arrangement whereby the difference between the higher costs of an American new-building, and those of other yards in Europe, Japan or elsewhere, was loaned to the shipowner by a branch of the American government, the U.S. Maritime Administration. But the design of the ship

Like London buses, States Line ships arrived in batches.

and its trade routes were subject to approval by that same government. This restriction, together with a similar operational subsidy, had the effect of limiting the size and world-wide scope of America's merchant fleet, while augmenting the essential quality of it. The early war-built 'Victory' ships had evolved into a larger version, the C1. The moth balled C2s, now reactivated, had enlarged to later C3s and then came the C4 'Mariners' with States Line operating the C4lSU 'Mariner' class. These self-sustaining ships incorporated six large holds, with two intermediate decks, flush throughout for fork lift operation. At each hatch, there were booms which could be instantly rigged for twenty ton lifts. All running gear was electrically operated, and all hatch openings, which were compact and 'slimline' of high tensile steel, were operated hydraulically. The ships were fast, all of them were engined by more than adequate steam turbines.

The States Line fleet made regular trans-Pacific voyages from the West coast to Hong Kong, Manila, Taiwan and Japan as well as the war zones around Saigon. The trade was a cut-throat one, becoming more so with the advent of containers. There were still some advantages to be found in the conventional 'break-bulk' carrier and my chief function as an operations man was to make these more effective. My main concerns were the stowage of the cargo with a nicely judged balance between the cost of labour used and quick despatch. There was also to arrange the vessel's port rotation while in the Sound, calling at Bellingham, Everett, Tacoma and Seattle's three berths, without backtracking. Plenty of room for mistakes existed. But, coming from foreign parts, and ripe for further fashioning, they allowed me a certain leeway, an exonerating neutrality. And in the unvoiced opinion of the little knot of union men who held sway down on the piers, I was accepted with an easy grace. They referred to me, lightly, but behind my back, as 'Captain Bligh.' My Seattle boss, Frank Swain, a tall Californian, advised me after a month that I 'stood tall' among the States Line's Captains and Officers. After the first year, the Management summoned me to San Francisco, travelling in style on board one of the ships, in order to show myself at their main office on California Street, and we wined and dined at Fisherman's Wharf. At home, all my girls were a hit with the neighbours up on 50th.Avenue N.E. Everything was going swimmingly.

For most of the time. Overweening ambition did, however, result in disaster, after loading our vessel *Illinois*, at Fisher's old berth, in Seattle. Two thousand tons of bagged flour lay waiting. Fisher's flour people had preserved their own antiquated warehouse and dock close to the centre of town. Large amounts of flour were shipped out world wide, mostly as aid to starving communities. 'Hands across the sea', depicting two joined hands, was the logo stencilled in red upon the small white cotton flour-sacks, piled high in every corner.

Low earning cargo such as this demanded lower costs of loading. With full sized gangs of sixteen men at each hatch for loading, any gains the shipowner might have achieved became minimal. But someone had to ship the stuff. The word from our boss in San Francisco was writ large, we did not need telling,

'Please do your utmost to cut down on labour costs.' Unbreakable contracts with the stevedores' union had long been cast, which would never agree to any reduction to the sixteen man gang. The International Longshore Workers Union was, for the most part, created and nurtured by Harry Bridges, a sworn communist, which was not a favoured political colour in the States at the time. This wily yet feisty character had survived extradition orders against him, and had been imprisoned after defying government edicts. He was as adroit in hatching his union intrigues as were his mafia counterparts who ran different unions on the East Coast, and the Gulf. There had been an occasion when he engineered a spurious strike, halting the ships from Long Beach to Alaska and gaining a full withdrawal of labour by the union locals; so that two days later when he made a fine speech calling it off, he would reveal himself as a friend of the employer, thereby winning further concessions. But he looked favourably on new work methods as sustaining a profitable workplace for his men. In recent negotiations he had permitted us to reduce the gang size, but only conditionally, to six men, introducing the 'robot' gang. This method involved loading the cargo on pallets, with fork-lift trucks down the hold, from cages which travelled with the cargo hook. On board the

— AMERICAN DREAM —

*My troubled friend **Illinois**.*

Illinois, at Fishers we allocated six robot gangs, and three gangs of full size. She could never have handled more.

Our regular night and day supercargoes disagreed with me. My helper on the day shift, Norm.Hansen, an affable spirit, but a man of few words said, merely, 'It aint gonna work at Fishers.'

John Cvitkovic, a voluble and excitable Serb, who took over as my man on the night side, gave strident voice. 'They'll be fallin' over themselves in the biggest jam you ever saw, just see if they don't,' he advised.

There had to be a way, I was sure. Friends in San Francisco would have told me so. Three full sized gangs, we agreed, would load by hand into the narrow ends of the ship. The six robots would pile up their pallets in the square spaces. At Fishers, the old wooden pier was in the style of the traditional American dock. In servicing nine gangs there was a great deal of congestion in the warehouse, as John predicted. Spilt flour had glossed the boards like talcum on a dance floor, and the trucks slithered their way to the cages waiting. The fork-lifts filled the warehouse with unbreathable blue diesel fumes. But slowly, the rhythm of regular loads arriving at the hook hustled on an ever more speedy rate. The ship finished her loading in the allotted time.

But this was not the end. *Illinois* was a ship that completed her loading to the south, in Californian ports, so that our flour stowage was kept to half empty holds, each face of which must be secured before sailing. In every hold there was a wall of pallets, twenty feet in height and from side to side. This made work for many more men in high cost extra labour. They built fences, shored up with 'A' frames of 6"x 4" timbers. This took half a day longer. And then she sailed, into a storm.

Square pallets and the sheer sweep of a ship's side do not lie well together. As the ship laboured her way down towards Cape Blanco, at each lurch the pallets closed up the gaps between, until the whole mass swayed in a body, to every roll. The fences broke asunder. Pallets fell to the floor, in a disordered heap. The flour sacks burst, spilling white breadflour over all the hold's floor, mixed with splintered pallet wood..

Illinois was bound down for Long Beach. When she opened her hatches a desolating sight met their eyes, and a great deal of labour was used, cleaning up the mess. There were no more robot gangs at Fishers after that, my very own disaster.

The States Line ships, like London buses, (there were eight of them in the fleet,) entered port in ungovernable batches, then abruptly left us with a number of rarified free days. During these periods I was able to leave the office early and take long enjoyable weekends at home, with my family.

Tow-boat companies generated a lot of income earned from berthing our ships. My colleague, Dick Horn, and I managed well for free lunches thereby, and in the summer, Foss Tugs would lay on their special boat for an office party cruise. The 'cruise ship' was an ageing steam yacht which had belonged to Douglas Fairbanks, the Hollywood star. She was a comely craft, finished in rich teak and shining brass, and cheerfully bore our pressing load of office staff, men, wives and spinsters, together with a stock of picnic food and beverages. The cruise, a quiet evening upon Lake Washington, started in sedate style, but grew noisier as the night advanced. My wife sat close to me, as it it was her first experience of the office women, mostly 'of an age.' Later in the evening Dick Horn, in a characteristic display of warmth, grabbed her by the waist, having been impressed by her undiluted English. He was a stocky little fellow from West Virginia, of shorter stature than she, 'And you – you're my Piccadilly girl!' he loudly declared.

Dick, with his easy, cheery manner could, more successfully than I, manage the cupidity of the Military Sealift Command. The grey civil servants of MSC controlled military cargoes, out at their own dock, Pier 91. Unlike commercial shippers who paid by the ton, MSC paid in advance for a total amount of ship space, in cubic feet, and then filled it with whatever cargo pleased them. Phone lines ran hot over which particular slice of space they were allotted. The loading areas of the ship varied. Some were accessible and easy and could take the cargo offered up to them, others were not.

We tried to beat the containerships.

So that demands which would have done credit to a Shylock were launched, with the military insisting that this tween deck or that particular lower hold end was quite naturally theirs to carve up without regard to adjacent parts. This would destroy my own carefully planned pre-stowages. They, as 'special customers' usually won.

On the other hand, I was the obvious choice at the time of a longshoremen's strike in Seattle, when the Canadian port of Vancouver remained treacherously working. I was despatched to the latter place. My instructions were to somehow persuade the Canadians to get our cargo moving south, across the border, speedily, by road. This was an impossible demand as I very quickly found out, and driving down to the dock, in my own American 'Chevvy' with Seattle plates, was greeted at an intersection by a head at a rolled down window shouting, 'Go home, Yank!'

For any activity not naturally American, I was the one selected, which I chose to take as a compliment. When we were appointed as owner's agents for the first Russian ship to enter the Port of Seattle since pre-war days, I was despatched on board. The M.V *Orsha* arrived from Vladivostock. She was shoddier than our own ships and slim built, there was an echo to the footstep that suggested an inferiority in her scantlings. Free passage on board had been restricted by the U.S Coast Guard. However, when I stepped up to the captain's dayroom, I found it filled with senior officials from Customs and

Immigration, the Port, the U.S.Navy, and avid reporters from the Seattle '*Times*' and '*Post Intelligencer.*' My own modest mission was to see to the ship's daily needs, a doctor or dentist for the crew, appoint a ship chandler, deliver the mail, set up any fresh water requirements, and send off the captain's arrival messages. The captain, who possessed little English, was a huge man dressed in a silver grey lounge suit. He dominated the small floor space that remained. Like a performing bear he stood, nodding and dipping affably, a bottle of neat vodka in his hand with which he charged, and recharged, our thimble glasses despite it being only just past eight in the morning. On the way down I stopped by the Chief Officer's cabin, for that is where the heart of the ship lay. A clean cut, honest man, I noted at leaving, and I fell into making comparisons. The subject was something to be reckoned with. I concluded that Russian officers were not unlike other Europeans, competent enough but strained by convention and regulation, the repression coming out of them in a number of individual ways. American officers did not seem to operate under similar restraints. Despite the image of 'cowboys' thrown at them by some, I found the States Line men to be unobtrusively self-assured, achieving professional standards that their counterparts in Europe would have done well to copy. In my private little assessment I considered modern Europeans inherited a lot of 'top hamper' from their stuffed-shirt sailor ancestors. American seafarers were not so burdened. They were more down to earth, having instead, a little of the Boston Cape Horner about them.

We had some lovable Captains. Brown was one, a little round man, not black, but nearly so, with a widening horizontal smile and crinkly hair in sparse quantities. With a gentle jerk of the head, and a secretive smile, he would dangle the question,

'Coming up for a heave ahead?' (a small scotch.)

Walter Day was a large boney individual having strong opinions about the job, and a fiery temper which he would let loose at me or anybody, but quickly recovering. We got on well. He continually inveighed to me about British cars which, he maintained, lacked sufficient coats of paint. We would take Chinese lunches ashore on an expense account.

John Beale was another broadly displayed character from Portland in Oregon, whose nervous habit of snorting and spitting discouraged any attempts at friendship. He ate, reminding me that I would benefit greatly from doing the same, hominy grits for breakfast, a meal in which I frequently joined him, aboard the *Washington* at Pier 20, taking care to order my eggs 'over-easy.' The keen young Captains we never saw. They stayed down in California, where the company had introduced a newer ship design, in an attempt to compete with container ships. These vessels would serve, they said, both the demand for containers and the conventional 'break bulk' cargoes, and sailed direct from San Francisco for the East. Their chief difference was in their hatches,

— American Dream —

now divided into three abreast, giving more direct loading access. The *Colorado* was the first. One great error was made in her design. The standard container, at inception a box 8 feet high, had in a few places, over a period of time, grown to 8 feet 6 inches. The deckhead space on *Colorado* would take eight feet only, with little to spare. This was the beginning of the end for States Line.

The Japanese had become the world leaders in trade, and in heavy industry there were few to beat them. Their well-equipped yards delivered container ships for new owners in every country which had understood their dominance, and these more efficient ships carried most of the cargoes into and out of that country.

There was, perhaps, something I did not know, the aspirations of our board room remained a closed book to me, but States Line never did convert to containers. They planned and built a roll-on/ roll-off vessel, the *Maine*, a wonder of expensive construction, but we never saw her in Seattle, and she was given over to the military, as a 'white elephant.' Our regular berth in the Port of Seattle, Pier 20, remained busy, large amounts of toys and plastic flowers from Hong Kong and Taiwan, were flooding in, and looking for ships whether container type or not. But our cargoes out were reduced to a trickle.

At Tacoma one day, there lay a Blue Star ship. As I left one of my ships to go home, I saw her there at an older pier. Blue Star Line were British, and rarely came this way. They were one of the first companies to haul chilled beef from the Argentine, and now worked world-wide as refrigerated carriers. This new arrival marked a revival of an old line, running from Australasia and the Pacific islands eastwards to Long Beach, San Francisco, and now Tacoma. From training ship days, I remembered these ships and their striking design, a low clean sleek look and, as they emerged from the mists of Long Reach, the oversized, overpowering orange funnel emblazoned with a huge blue star. They made their stately way up to the Royal Docks, coming from goodness knows where, and we ogled them, determined one day to join one.

It was none of my business, quite the opposite, in fact, but something persuaded me to stop the car under the shadow of that orange stack. Uneasily I climbed her gangway, not knowing what I would find. I entered her living spaces, long cream painted alleyways with closed doors, festooned overhead with a collection of running pipes. There was nobody about. The lower decks were tiled, with, in the corners, long standing piles of British dust. As I climbed I reached the carpeted levels. Thrilled feelings of a revisited past ran warmly through me. I found suddenly that I was as excited as a child at a school picnic. Then rose familiar, the very familiar smells, for it was nearly high tea time. Now, with surer footsteps I came upon the little corner bar, harbouring a cigarette smoke cloud and a row of sturdy Englishmen, hugging their cans. Diffidently, I introduced myself, as they had fallen silent at the sight of my grey suit and white shirt with sober tie. The Captain appeared unannounced, a stockier facsimile of his officers, and a richer shade of puce, but possibly seeing something of the Captain Browett about me disappeared again. Weakly, I offered a personal history, I hoped to interest them. In this I failed. They did not seem to care that I picked from a pile on a small table, an edition of the Merchant Navy Officers' Association newspaper. The headline was unmissable,

'GET YOUR UNIFORM OUT OF MOTHBALLS' it challenged. 'The sea life is calling you back!'

The British Merchant Service was, in a way, getting its just desserts. Officers, deeply discouraged at the lack of prospects, had exited in large numbers. And now, with ships laid up for lack of officers, the companies were pleading. They should give up their shore jobs, and return, the paper cried. Augmented pay, and quick promotion were promised in oversized company matrixes. There were some glamourised ship pictures in colour. I took some old editions home with me. My wife watched with careful eyes as I poured over them and devoured the advertisements, turning the pages continuously.

We shared added domestic worries. Drugs at the girls' school had not yet spread their evil miasma over our home, but had moved dangerously close. The war and the Watergate affair created overheated public unease. Whenever I left a ship in the night now, coming home I opened the vodka bottle, persuading Judy Gray to join me. We drank far too much, and it started to affect our lives. Even my lady Seattle was at a dip in her fortunes as a city. Boeing made no planes. House prices were sharply down.

'Will the last person to leave,' they said, 'please turn out the lights?'

In the same style as many of our fateful, really big family decisions this one plopped out in the tiredness of the night, without preamble or reasoned argument. My ship at Pier 20, *Illinois*, had sailed down the Sound loaded nearly to her marks with alfalfa pellets in bulk, pulp in bales, and walnut logs with which the Japanese would veneer their pianos. The night was well advanced. Judy Gray was waiting up, she always did. The living room was bathed in television blue. An old English movie was showing. There were 'bobbies' with pointy helmets. A sickly dose of lumpy throated homesickness followed, with copious tears. Then we decided. We had never found our roots here in this new country, for we had left it too late. So it was back to Britain, all of us.

We were not the last to leave Seattle. We did not switch off any lights. In fact I carried a heart's glimmer with me, and still do, for that grand and beautiful city. I carried it aboard the big 747, and down through all the years.

Chapter Eleven

LOSS OF DOSS

There comes a time, as everyone knows, for putting away childish things. Seemingly, I had not yet reached it although I was now well past the age of forty. As we dropped towards Heathrow I had suffered the excitement of a child. A pattern of English meadows, sectioned into shades of green by reddish suburban blocks had emerged from a layer of thin cloud below me. I felt an excess of warm possessive pride – a consequence of my absent seven years. And with it, the germ of an idea, a means of capturing the moment, an idea silly in the extreme. It was, after taxiing to a stop – to lay my forehead on the tarmac, as a gesture of love and pride in regaining my native soil. It never happened, of course. We were bundled from the dense brightness of the plane's interior onto a darkened blue walkway, far above any tarmac, and hustled along plastic passages without the slightest whiff of English air. The euphoria of being back stayed with me for some time, creating, in the figurative sense, a flexing of the muscles, firing up my ambition for another 'great forge ahead.'

Judy and the girls had not had the same gratifying experience. They had arrived weeks ahead of me, on an earlier flight. This arrangement, however disagreeable, was preferred, as best suited to our financial limitations. Once again, she had the worst of it, and she bore up stoically. She had not yet seen our household effects and most of her things which were *en route,* stowed to our own plan in a twenty foot container and shipped aboard the Danish vessel *Meonia*. With the three girls, she was squeezed into a cramped set of rooms at our parents' home town of Gloucester, where she waited with as much patience as she could muster for me to commence our search for, and purchase of, a new home. The dogs, suitably sedated, had flown in the cargo hold on the same plane and they were now quarantined. But the three girls had found things not in accord with their eager hopes. They were too young to have harboured any sweeter recollections, and, not surprisingly, behaved as Americans coming to live in a strange land. The English spoke 'funny,' their streets were medieval in size, and seen from the train the contracted fields, reduced by so many hedgerows, were over-populated with brown or black and white cattle. The fetor of the public lavatories nauseated. Cagey-looking shoppers trudged homeward dangling their groceries in droopy plastic bags – so different from the tall brown paper ones that you hugged in your encircling arms, comfortingly crackling. The absence of wall-to-wall carpets and drinking faucets in the schools was noisily deplored. Settling in, for them, was going to take some time.

Getting onto a shipowner's payroll was a priority for me, but a *role* into which I slid easily, and with some relish. Directly from the airport, I made my way to the Shipping Federation in Aldgate. Everything I had heard was true. The feeling was to have been grabbed at the door, without release until I committed myself to a ship. There were plenty of these to choose from.

'How quickly can I expect a command?' my first question burst out before any interview had found a footing. For some inexplicable reason, I had not communicated with Furness, but having been offered a wide spread of dubious tramp ships, the common sense of the idea became clear. The Federation man placed his phone in front of me, to dial. Instantly, I recognised the voice at the other end, as he did mine.

'Is that you, Mr. Cater?' I cried, needlessly.

They gave me back most of my seniority and proposed, with caution, that I could expect my own command in eighteen months to two years, as long as the fleet strength remained the same. With a consideration which I thought unnecessary, they appointed me as a supernumerary Chief Officer for a few weeks, until I 'found my feet.'

Furness Withy, as a corporate structure, had changed. The buoyant body of busy shipping companies had sold off a good portion of their ageing tonnage, and diversified a little. But as they would have said, a leaner and fitter line of ships had emerged. The container revolution, and the economic pressures giving birth to it, had been the main cause. Yet the company's original lines were still active in reduced form. They had also branched out into the intermediate trades, with the Cairn Line. A modern new fleet of small bulk carriers, (no-one dared to refer to them as coasters) looked for business at any and every port from Scandinavia to the Central Mediterranean. The company's assets ashore, which included ship terminals, stevedoring and intermodal transport added to its attraction for a take-over by any other container group.

– Loss Of Doss –

The 'Cairn boats', no-one dared to call them coasters.

One of the ageing beauties of Shaw Savill's fleet became the first to receive me as a supernumerary Chief Officer. She was the *Illyric*, newly arrived at Southampton, and carrying lamb and butter from New Zealand in frozen loose stowage. I marched up to Captain Buller's room, to introduce myself.

'Good morning, Sir, ' I offered, in the breezily cheerful tones I had learned to adopt in the uncertain atmosphere of a strange captain's dayroom. I explained my presence, and how I came to be there. This was a mistake. I was greeted with frostiness. The Captain, dumpy and pear-shaped possessed a red face, which now, in the silence, coloured to a deeper crimson. I was a lowly Chief Officer, still. You did not go up to 'shoot the breeze' with captains. You went on board to prowl the decks and see to the well-being of the vessel.

I was at least invited up at Sunday G.& T. time. We had, after Southampton, touched in at a spread of North Sea ports as far as Oslo. It was in the nature of our frozen cargo to distribute small shipments in many places, according to the market. On the Sunday in question, a sunny morning crossing at speed the sparkling waters of the Skagerrak, all seniors, including the North Sea pilot were invited to gin and tonics with the Captain before lunch.

As a sure sign of changing days, the smaller Cairn boats were leaving builders' yards in Holland and Germany. A deeply reforming new agreement had been thrashed out on manning, allowing a reduction of the crew to thirteen men. (The average number at that time for a standard cargo ship was between forty and fifty.) New divisions of labour were devised. Deck Officers were reduced from three to two, besides the Master. The Mate and Second would now perform 'watch and watch', i.e., six hours on and six hours off, a tiring round but one for which a short-hand bonus was paid. And, urgently, from ship to ship the enquiry passed – would we exchange our bed linen, (sheets, blankets and counterpane embroidered with the company's *motif*) for a warming duvet? There would be no bed to make, as there was no steward to make them. Meals were to be drawn from the cook, forming a line outside the galley.

When the moment came, my first reappointment happened to be similar in size to the Cairn Line vessels, yet so very different. Brian Cater, the man in sea personnel who held my fate in his hands, was becoming impatient.

'When *will* you be ready, then?' he asked, a little plaintively. I had been forced to stall. We still had not found a new home. There was some difficulty in obtaining a mortgage, as my years spent wilfully out of the country implied insecurity. Eventually we found a future home in Devon. The paper-work was not quite done, when Brian called me for a ship. I had been on full pay, doing relieving work. I pleaded for more time.

'Just a couple of weeks more,' I said, 'and I should be ready to go away.'

'O.K., *we'll* find you something,' he said, downing the phone firmly. And he did. She was one of the small ones, with a crew of thirteen, but a different proposition altogether from one of the Cairn Line 'little bulkies.' *Bergen Juno* was a 'Hustler', a baby container ship. She had long ago left behind the Norwegian fjord which had named her and now traded within the Caribbean. She was chartered to an American fruit company, and carried bananas and bags of coffee in forty-foot containers, from Guatemala up into New Orleans. Outward, she called at Port Royal, Jamaica and Puerto Barrios in Honduras, with general cargo.

Suddenly I was airborne once more, and in a very short time rediscovered America in the form of a close, hot and clammy New Orleans, Louisiana, known in the trade as 'Nola.'

I stood on the dock and watched *Bergen Juno* come in. She skidded stern-first and arrow straight down the fairway, an exemplary performance due to her bow thruster propeller operated by a well practised pilot. Nothing I had ever seen was quite like this. With a rear end square, unlovely and black, she was disfigured by a hole in the middle of it, blocked off by a portcullis similar to the up-and-over door of a garage. But the door dropped, like a bascule bridge. An officer had walked aft and operated an outside button, at which the whole thing hinged down onto the dockside ramp, landing with a grinding boom close to where I was standing. This action stripped away enough of the stern to reveal her main deck, which was stowed three high with containers. Hidden from view, on railway tracks which ran the length of the ship, was the portal crane, making her independent of dockside facilities. But before I could take in more of this new vision before me, high above the dock I heard a shout. Leaning a wild and gingery head over the high deck rail which formed a lintel to the 'hole in the stern', a crazed individual attached to a matted rust-coloured beard was calling loudly, and appeared to be drunk. I could not make out what he was saying, for the words were abusive in nature, yet addressed in quite friendly style to a quietly dressed gentleman whom I took to be the agent, standing close to me. The voice belonged to Captain Campbell, a Royal Mail lines master who had been removed to *Bergen Juno* from the big ships. This must be a bad boys' ship, I concluded – or perhaps he was just tired. (The ship took the more tedious route into New Orleans, through a chain of canals, dug through flat green bayous, an option taken to relieve traffic congestion on the Mississippi.) Ignoring the abuse, the agent and I made for a narrow casing and the stairs up to the higher deck, which small area, I found, contained all the living accommodation. The steel casing also walled in the engine room door, left open for relative coolness, but the suffocatingly hot interior was filled with diesel fumes. I reached the cabin door of the man whom I had come to replace. Campbell was by then prowling the alleyways, but stopped dead as he clapped eyes on me. Then he moved up more closely. He silently inspected me from top to toe and then uttered the first words he ever addressed to me.

'I hope you can drive that fucking crane,' he said.

This came as a surprise. I was unfamiliar with any ships possessing a crane. And even more so with the art of driving one. Fortunately, this only happened in the outports, American safety rules would never have permitted an untrained amateur to manipulate the thing. I had at least the time, until loading containers of coffee commenced, to learn the ropes. But only after my shipmate, Chris Fazakerly, our second officer, became exhausted with a six hour spell incarcerated in the tiny cab, could I persuade myself to go up and relieve him. In the sticky heat of Puerto Cortes, the cab resembled an oven.

'It's quite simple, really,' Chris squeezed over to offer me the little leather pad of a seat. 'Two levers. One for lift and lower. The other for traversing the crane, just look down from time to time to see that longshoremen are not standing on the tracks, sometimes the alarm throws a wobbler.'

By means of a square frame fitted with twist locks I clamped onto each container. The jerky motion was difficult to control, particularly with the twenty-odd ton weight of a loaded container swinging gently. It took a little practice. After the first four hours it became easier and I found that I was beginning to enjoy it, just like any small boy. Each truck and trailer with its container drove up the stern ramp, and along the deck, until I sited the crane above it. The trucks were the big American ones, with the exhaust chimneys protruding vertically from the rear side of the cab. With a spirited rhythm I filled up the slots of a hold, replacing the heavy steel lid as if boxing off a tin of biscuits, and airily continued to pile the boxes on deck.

By the third round trip, driving the crane had become part of the job.

Until we lost the brakes. Those brakes! That day, suddenly they seemed a mite spongey – or could it be my imagination? No, impossible! The container was walking back while I held it suspended. Quickly, quickly, now, do the only thing, for it was right over the driver in his cab! Full Speed! We, the crane, container and I bore away up the deck at an outlandish rate, guillotining the truck's exhaust chimney at its stump and sending the dock gangs running for cover; while the half dozen or so grey-garbed Guatemalan soldiers who lounged around all day with submachine guns slung across their chests, sprang to the alert.

It was a fairly regular occurence, they said. Fixers were forever flying out from the makers in Germany – this was a most temperamental crane. Even the wires behaved erratically. Frequently, when winding onto the drum, these ultra-flexible wires rode over one another and jammed, causing work stoppages. I was sorry I ever had to sail with the thing. We were lucky to have a versatile bosun and a crew from Barbados, drawn from local schooner men. They had a happy knack with cranes.

But the uncertain container weights were my concern. For more than a year the ship had carried the boxes, filled by heavy coffee bags, with their weights 'approximate,' in the uppermost tier. In less backward countries the regular use of an accurate weighbridge would have been compulsory. A vessel similar to ours had recently capsized with all hands, in the South Atlantic, for reasons that seemed to be obscure. On our next arrival in 'Nola' I drew aside the agent and made a plea for more control, at Puerto Cortes. He understood my concern, and would 'do what he could,' he said. But more than my mere suspicions were needed to change the ways of a lucrative trade.

Campbell offered no help, neither would he accept any. We had agreed, tacitly, to go our separate ways, as this was better than simmering warfare. He took pride in his seamanship and ship handling which he approached in the same way as a game of Russian roulette. If he could miss hitting a tempting navigational danger, by just skirting it, he was showing consummate skill. On one of his more boisterous evenings, we awaited a pilot in order to sail from Puerto Barrios. The pilot was late, and Campbell determined to sail by himself, an act prohibited. He should have managed, but misjudged the wind effect, and before the anchors were up, the ship swung full circle, landing hard upon an adjacent ship. The point of contact was in the area of our bridge, where a quick-release lifebuoy was positioned. The buoy had its smoke flare attached, and the compressive contact set alight the flare, befogging the scene with billowing orange smoke. Campbell stood, centred in a Dante's Inferno, wreathed in the smoke tinted by the evening's pinkish light to a poisonous orange, while frothing curses through his grinding teeth.

As an addition to his wife, Campbell had attached himself to a lady at home to whom he made long calls on the bridge radio phone, sometimes bursting into romantic song, despite members of the watch on bridge duty close by. One of his indulgences was to fly the lady out to New Orleans, to be there, on our arrival. Our regular ship chandler, a swarthy Mexican (and Campbell's sole aider and abettor), would meet and install her in one of the French quarter hotels. Grandly, the words 'Ship's Providor' headed the pages of his account with the Owners. His bills, countersigned by Campbell, were grossly inflated in order to cover the lady's excursions, and a candle light dinner for two would appear on the account as a sufficiency of best beef. We stood to benefit. Campbell's favourite dish at the saloon table was Louisiana prawns basking in a split avocado, of which we all partook, bribed to quietness thereby. But these wildly excessive bills could never have passed scrutiny in London and reports were feeding back, as they always did.

Campbell was relieved, and repatriated. A young 'rookie' took over, and shortly afterward my tour of duty expired, a total of four months. This was one of the real 'plusses'. Lengthy leaves at home with my wife had become a regular feature.

Once a small ship man, always a small ship man, that's how it struck me, then. I liked them well enough, and in the office, from some disembodied source, they had learned this. But only the little Cairn Line ships appealed, the Hustlers no longer did. 'Cairnboats' traded close to home, and regular phone calls brought us closer. There was the short-hand bonus. Besides, the hands on procedures where our own methods were of value gave a lot of satisfaction. On these ships I could, and did, dig out my thick seaboot socks and boots, and lead my three sailors below. With a brush on a pole, we applied a coat of whitewash to holds in preparation for salt cargoes, and similar workaday projects. Also, I reasoned, master of the little ships was likely to be a position more attainable for me. Sailing away to azure tropic seas was not within their scope. The *Cairnrover* was time chartered to a Swedish concern having its main office in Lidköping, a small town on Lake Vanern. She carried her cargoes from there to places on the wintry Baltic coasts. In order to access the lake, she must pass through the port of Gothenburg, and transit the Trollhattan canal, verily a place of trolls as we silently passed at night through virgin woods, coming upon small fairyland locks which loomed out of shadows as if from nowhere.

In the lake we came to Otterbäken, a town of industrial bleakness. Piled on the dock were black heaps of zinc concentrates, muddy with rain and dusted with snow. Every ten day voyage we transported a load of this, in bulk, to the Belgian port of Antwerp. A load surprisingly full of danger, for two trips previously it had very nearly capsized *Cairnrover*. On the open dock the sodden heaps of concentrates lay through the winter, forming black puddles. On that fateful trip, she had taken on her load as the heavy rain continued. She gained open water, but after rounding the Skaw had encountered rough seas, and commenced to roll, heavily. The cargo, still sodden and in a syrup-like suspension, formed waves and started to heave. My shipmate, George Smith, the Chief Engineer, was there when it happened, and entered the hold through a 'booby hatch.'

'It surged, and changed direction like some berserk amphibian out of pre-history,' he related, afterwards. A two thousand ton amphibian. When, by some accident of mechanics, it came to rest, the mass had shuffled to one side producing a most dangerous, and permanent, list. The Master put into the Danish port of Esbjerg as a port of refuge, thankful to lie so close. The cargo was restowed and dried.

The event created a blizzard of M notices, put out by H.M. Stationery Office, covering *Cairnrover* with fame. But we were not the first ship. Colliers leaving the port of Swansea with wet shifting slurry had sunk. It was just that we were a 'well found' vessel, well managed and immune from such disasters. A device that was new to all of us, a moisture-tester, came aboard in an expensive beechwood box. But, mindful of the sailors' disdain to use such gimmicks, management instituted a whimsical testing device. Now, each time we came to Otterbäken, it was decreed, we must take a tin can and half-fill it, from the pile on the dock, with concentrates. This must then be taken below to the engine room and placed on top of the generator in use, which vibrated at a steady rate. The action separated off some water that shivered in the can, after rising to the top. If this water was excessive, the cargo's moisture content was thereby proved to be too high and we must refuse to load it. It was my great good fortune never to be encumbered with this decision. The shippers had ensured by then, that only dry cargo was allowed to sit on the dockside, by the simple expedient of covering it with tarpaulins when it rained.

The run was a triangular one. From Antwerp we proceeded through the Kiel Canal to Riga, in Latvia. Here we loaded back coal, for any port in Sweden. While in Antwerp, a companionable captain, a 'good sort' took over. This was 'Lawn-mower Lloyd' so named in respect of his unwieldy way of walking, and waving his feet about, like cylinder-mower blades, before they found the deck. Bertie (his real name) was as strange to the Cairn line ships and runs as I was. But not for long, the Baltic was about to give up its secrets.

– Loss Of Doss –

It was winter-time at iron-curtained Riga, and the ice lay thick in the Gulf. *Cairnrover* was, like all the 'Cairns' underpowered, and quite quickly became stuck in it. This alarmed poor Bertie beyond measure, and everyone else by association. We should have had sense enough to recognise the likelihood, for every merchant ship operating in the Baltic that season steamed around with her hull paint at the waterline removed by the abrasive contact and the steel beneath polished to a high bright silver. But that was not the worst of it. The icefield, having no visible boundary and without life in any form, made a friendless, barren place. We lay there, marooned. Denizens of the west who spoke only English into their transmitters were properly ignored. After three days of Bertie's unanswered urgency messages, a battered old steam tug came out, circled round us to break up the ice, and escorted us inward. Even then the Bolshevik cold shoulder greeted us. Armed guards dressed in the Russian style conducted ship inspections, both on arrival and at departure. While every crew member was mustered in the dining room searches were made in all the others, under beds and into cupboards, for undesirables. While alongside in the port, we were allowed visits to only one place, and that was by dedicated bus to avoid strays. This was the International Seaman's Club where we could play billiards and table tennis or buy cut glass and copper samovars at the tax-free shop. At the counters, Marxist principles were dispensed with. American dollars were grabbed unceremoniously, and later privately exchanged in the street, at a flourishing black market rate. There were hostesses who sat with us and made much of their country's lifestyle. When asked if they ever visited other places abroad, we were quickly hushed, and they peered carefully over their shoulders to see who could be listening.

Cairnrover was a regular on that Baltic coast and we touched in at the old ports of the Hanseatic league, Gdansk (or Danzig), Stettin and Rostock, all full of dark shadows and perpetual gloom from the war's terrible aftermath, with their peoples still cowed by the Russian bear.

Bertie Lloyd and I made the round of the Cairn Line fleet, together and separately. We fitted well together. Many of our ships worked their way into the Western Mediterranean with fixings made on the Baltic Exchange, such as rape seed from Bordeaux to Algiers. In the Western Med. cargoes homeward could be found easily. The most common of these was simple sea salt, to be found in drying pans in Cagliari, Sardinia and Port de Bouc at the mouth of the Rhone. Norway consumed a great deal of the stuff, which it stockpiled for use on ice-bound roads, and we obligingly deposited it in ports as far North as Tromso, navigating the fjords' inner leads. In this way the maximum shelter could be found from frequent storms. We sailed hundreds of miles 'inside' wherever they formed a part of our route, mostly under pilotage, to any port north of Bergen.

I was with Bertie again on the *Soldier Prince* – one small container ship alone was keeping Prince Line's flag valiantly visible in the Eastern Med. She carried only containers to the few links remaining open to free and safe trading. At the Turkish port of Iskenderun, a trunk road now carried our containers direct to Baghdad. Lattakia had changed its arab face. Once one of Syrian friendship where the agent had given presents, to me a dress length of Damascus silk for my wife. Now, a new generation with an adolescent fierceness were readied for war. In place of a tranquil anchorage we found new concrete breakwaters, and quays patrolled by Russian-built military equipment. And old Beirut without its French-speaking Arab Christians, so flashily wealthy, was also now a battleground staked out by high-rises full of bullet holes.

When Bertie left, an end came to the lunch time challenge. Each day, when I came down from the bridge at noon, there was beer to be drunk. Two cans per man, in the payer's cabin, by strict rotation, Bertie, the Chief and I. The game was to miss a turn, and Bertie was best at it. Each day, he would cry,

'Whose turn is it today?' implicitly removing himself from the fray.

On one of my 'Cairns', the master (not Bertie) fell sick with a recurring illness, and took to his bed. He nominated me as his successor with little option to do otherwise.

Without mishap, the ship docked at her destination, Blyth, in Northumberland. This prompted one of my few letters to management. In it I poured out my frustrations. I had some seniority now, and enough competence, was it not time I was given a master's position? That was all I needed to say, I was aware, by this time, of the slimness of my chances. Too many of the company's ships and jobs were going to second-hand buyers. Its trades were being taken over by foreign concerns far more enterprising. Significantly, they operated with cheaper crews, and were fully converted to containers.

While at home on leave, a letter summoned me to London. An appointment had been made for me with Brian and Captain Murray, a personnel superintendent. To my surprise, it was not I who was the supplicant. It was they who wanted something from me. The central office for personnel had been moved to King George V dock, in East London. They ushered me into a quiet corner, with a paper cup of coffee.

'You know of the *Kayeson*, Mr.Jones?' Captain Murray quietly questioned.

I did, but very little. At launching, *Kayeson* was one of the biggest supertankers of her day. Mammoth tankers, it needs to be said, of our present era which pass round the Capes as they are too big for the Suez or Panama, had not yet been conceived. *Kayeson*, floating out at 64,000 tons was of the original supertanker generation. She was now past middle age, and unpopular. There had been a time when everyone built a tanker or two. The ships were star earners in the 1960s when world-wide demands for oil exceeded the carrying capacity. Oil companies paid high salaries for men to sail

*The supertanker **Kayeson**
(reproduced by kind permission of the Furness Group archives).*

in their tankers. The ships were attractively appointed, all staircases and public rooms were spacious and lined with expensive veneers and officers' cabins for their time were exceptional, each with their own bathroom.

The others, and Furness Withy was one, paid a little less. They attracted only a few and those with some difficulty, as most men said that if they had wanted a tanker, they'd have joined a tanker company.

'We want you to sail as Chief Officer on the *Kayeson*, Captain Murray said. Only one regular man was left, and there must be two, alternating. The company would bear in mind, he said, my right to early promotion, by virtue of my seniority. It was arm-twisting of the nicest kind.

A course for the tanker safety certificate was arranged for me at the Warsash College near Southampton. Then I would understudy the present mate for six months, thereby acquiring the mandatory endorsement to my Master's 'ticket', all before I could take the job.

I soon found, as I needed to, how inadequate was learning about tankers from text books. There were many, including *Kayeson*, which by design could not comply with the rulebook's later refinements. One of these was 'inerting' where explosive gases were neutralised by pumping an inert gas into emptying cargo tanks. And, of course, there were tankers whose antiquated parts did not operate well, such as the *Kayeson*'s stripping pumps. A little knowledge made me even more dangerous.

I joined her in Houston, Texas, in the spring of 1978. This was her regular discharge port, where a full load of Mexican crude from Pajaritos was delivered each trip. *Kayeson* was on a milk run between the two ports. She commenced pumping on arrival and sailed on completion. Her Chief Officer was by habit and custom required to be on deck throughout. It was no easy matter, then, to emerge from the plane suddenly smitten by Texas humidity, jet lagged and red eyed, to take over the deck with hardly time enough to don an oil stained boiler suit and to smother one's self with insect repellant oil in order to liquidate the killing mosquitoes swarming on the still yellow waters of the San Jacinto river. The man to be relieved would have his homeward flight booked to go, and doubled hotel bills were not contemplated. But the lessons about dealing with crude oil were hardest of all. I soon learned that you must keep your nose and mouth away from the sulphurous stuff. This was not so simple, as when taking ullages, the action required a close inspection at the tank opening, coating the mouth's insides with an evil deposit of black.

The sludge left when tank cleaning, which was required between grades, was highly obnoxious. This cleaning was performed by Butterworth hoses lowered in stages down each of the twenty-three cargo tanks. The hoses ejected a pressure spray of steamy water that might increase the explosive mix, and was therefore strictly controlled. The crew were Somali, and I was fortunate in this as they did not shrink from entering the tanks with me, to remove the sludge.

Loading at four thousand tons per hour through three 'Chiksan' arms needed my strongest nerves due to the risk of overspill. This was made worse by the *Kayeson*'s wheel valves whose spindles were old, bent and damaged adding to the preciously brief time taken to shut off at my breathless signal. But discharging, with pumps not 100 per cent efficient caused the greatest problems. And becoming expert enough to understand their near-human idiosyncracies was something I never mastered. When, on a deviation from our usual run, we took on board an abnormally gassy type of crude in Skikda, Algeria for New Orleans, the discharge was found to be impossible and compressors were hired from the shore.

Repairs were on a make-do-and-mend basis. Our superintendent in charge of these flew out frequently from Liverpool, always having as his priority our extrication from any likely off-hire charges assessed by the charterer, the Shell company. Also, economy was uppermost in his mind. Heating coil pipes at the 'ceiling' of the cargo tanks needed frequent patching up. This was not possible without enough ladders to ascend to the top of the tanks. Our 'super's' suggestion was that, with a rubber dinghy that he would supply, we fill the tank with water enough to float under and make our own repair. One slight movement of the ship giving energy to a mass of moving water could have sent the dinghy's occupants to an early and unpleasant drowning, and I withdrew my cooperation at this suggestion.

Our captains alternated. They were both tanker men – a label which I have taken care to avoid. Ernie Gowland was a pink-faced explosive sort of man, but one with whom I happily saw eye to eye. He navigated with confidence. Occasionally we discharged at Mississippi refineries above New Orleans, which required at least one waiting anchorage. While I stood by the anchors right forward with my head in the river bank brushwood, Gowland would stick the bow into the soft lightbrown mud, in order to swing in as tight a circle as possible. This made me think about tankers with two 'skins'. Environmental damage from escaping oil, a result of tanker casualties, gave rise to demands for a second skin for tankers, making virtually two hulls. This has become the accepted new-building practice. *Kayeson* had only her original single bottom. But a sizable sharp rock sunk in that Mississippi mud would have pierced any number of skins should our cleaving bow have found it under the mud, making this safeguard, I considered, largely useless. Gowland was happy as long as his moorings alongside were kept bar tight. This was because the slightest ranging movement could conceivably fracture any connections our pipes had with the shore.

Ernie's relief, a Liverpool man named Cadbury suffered many frights from thunderstorms. These tropical downpours, with lightning, had been known to provoke massive explosions at oil terminals. During such times, which in the hurricane season were common, we shut down the operation.

Just a few parts per million of oil in our tank washing slops were permitted. We were allowed to pump the settled water part of these from our slop tank into the sea in designated areas of ocean many miles away from land. The oil should, if given time, have risen to the top. The interface between oil and water, however, was difficult to determine, even though we had, at our disposal, ingenious 'detectors.' It was hard to trust one's own judgement. I was made easy, therefore, when another officer on the ascending ladder became available, and I was offered an escape. The Owners of *Kayeson* were the subject of a Queen's award for export achievement in that year. We all received the token lapel badge and tie.

South America, in Furness boardroom terms, was divided between Pacific Steam Navigation Co., on the west, and Houlder Bros., on the east, both long established companies within the group. I had been appointed to the *Oropesa* for the west coast run down to Chile, but a change in plan redirected me to *Derwent*, the only general cargo trader running for Houlder Bros. to Brazil and Argentina. In its early days, Houlders had been a company of importance in Argentina. Their fleet of meat carriers, the 'Grange' ships, brought back to London full cargoes of Argentine beef, hung in chambers chilled but never frozen. The ships sometimes steamed at 'slow' in order to arrive with the meat at its prime condition. Old John Houlder had come down to the *Worcester* in my training ship days to present the 'Houlders oars', a silver trophy of crossed oars, to the winning division's rowing crew. So, a *Worcester* boy could feel at home on board *Derwent*.

She was an SD14, one of a brand new breed built 'on spec.' in large numbers, to fill a great need. Hundreds of war-built liberty ships had carried a large share of world trade but by the 70s all, or nearly all, were sadly departed, leaving a wide gap. The small beginnings of the 'Liberty' had been conceived in England, in a north eastern shipyard, and here the SD14 standard design had also originated. She was not beautiful. But *Derwent* was fitted out to a high standard, and her size was ideal for the run down to Rio, Santos and the River Plate. For her cargo operations she was fully self-sustaining, and she possessed one of the latest 'Stulken' heavy lift derricks for large loads.

We had our pick of surplus 'company men,' well used to the ships and the run, a result of the gradual run-down of the fleet. This proved to be a mixed blessing, as amongst my deck gang, which numbered twelve, there were two or three people who had devised over time unorthodox methods of augmenting their pay. My job, the way I saw it, was to practise some kind of order in the cost of labour. Some conflict between us resulted. Clever schemes had been incubated concerning extra overtime, by which a man's wage could be doubled. Work, which could have been performed in straight time, was not. There was, to be sure, enough of it. Outward bound all running gear needed to be overhauled and homeward the ship was thoroughly cleaned and painted. But the extra hours held an attraction. For example, if a man who was to be put on night watch on arrival at a port, had not previously rested for eight hours he could claim for 'loss of sleep' paid at overtime rates. My gang had it 'sewn up,' by nominating the one with the least rest, thereby gaining the biggest payment. I insisted that the one who had slept sufficiently got the job. This controversy swelled in importance, from trivial to bitter, and was never rectified. 'Loss of doss', so called, with its inevitable side effects, in turn damaged employer/union relations at a much higher level.

As well as men with inflexible opinions, there were men of ability, and this proved so with the *Derwent*'s catering staff. Smooth operators all, they kept an impeccable table in the saloon, very good cabin service and served up a rich menu. These extras encouraged me to take my wife away for a voyage. This was a recent privilege given to seniors, and our girls were grown-up now. After my leave, she joined with me in Liverpool, and we cruised the North and South Atlantic as far as Rio and on down to the River Plate. She was looked after by our cabin steward, George, who brought her morning coffee and tea and biscuits in the afternoon on full silver service every day, in fair weather and foul. George, with his soft pale skin and dark good looks, should have

– Loss Of Doss –

The generous bonus paid for our holiday in Majorca.

been a woman, and very nearly was when he dressed as one in his lonely sallies ashore at Rio Grande and Santos.

While Judy Gray was with me, we had a change from our usual homeward cargo for Liverpool, which consisted mainly of corned beef in twelve-pound tins. A complete departure from Houlders' preferred route was a fixture of bulk grain for Aalborg, in Denmark. This was waiting at San Lorenzo, above Rosario on the River Parana, a tributary of the Plate. We tied up to a wooden pier, far too small for us, but host to a horde of plump, grain-fed rats. The grain was poured through one fixed spout, so that in order to distribute it throughout the ship's length it became necessary to move the ship up or down, every couple of hours. This was an irksome chore, as the work continued through day and night, and, to move the ship all hands were required. Not only this, but the cargo was sub-divided into many different lots, each requiring a separate stowage. The problems were unique, and my learning years in Seattle served me well. The charterers awarded a generous bonus on completion, enough to help pay for a family holiday at the Club Galazzo on Majorca. Likewise, my deck gang ended their trip richer. Their 'loss of doss' earnings from nights spent shifting the ship for real, beat all expectations.

My last *Derwent* voyage ended in Hull after three months. In the interim, auspicious events had taken place in the world of takeovers. Furness Withy had been acquired, lock, stock and barrel by a Chinese gentleman. C.Y. Tung had come down to

Commemoration of christening, **Pacific Prestige**.

Hong Kong from Shanghai to escape the aftermath of Chairman Mao's ascendancy. He was already the owner of some shipping ventures, but extended them quickly in that most fruitful period. His new wealth enabled him to buy the elderly Cunarder *Queen Elizabeth*. In a play upon his name, he renamed her *Seawise University* and, in an act of philanthropy, turned her over to the authorities as an educational establishment. (Tragically, the vessel went on fire in Hong Kong harbour, and was totally lost.)

Furness Withy had wandered into his sights, as an afflicted company with rich assets. One of these was the established firm of Manchester Liners. An enterprising company, ML switched to container ships in time to maintain their hold over the transatlantic trade to Canada, from Manchester. And C.Y was then preparing to circle the globe with ships of the new Orient Overseas Containers Limited.

We were not yet a part of these vaunted plans. In fact, the fear of redundancy had spread gloom throughout the Furness fleet. No one knew what would happen to us. Evil rumours abounded, and word had it that the whole fleet was to be 'flagged out' with all the jobs going east.

Things turned out not quite so bad as that. There was good news to come from Brian Cater, while I was at home after *Derwent*.

'How'd you like a brand new ship?' he said.

The Tung group consisted of many ship types. Our side, it appeared, was to be awarded the management of six new bulk carriers and two tankers, at that moment building at different yards in Japan. They were all Panamax size, i.e., of the maximum permitted width (106 feet) to pass through the locks of the Panama Canal. Big ships, too, carrying a deadweight tonnage of 63,000 metric tons. I was assigned to one of these, as Chief Officer on the *Pacific Prestige*.

We were, in these new circumstances, introduced to an admirable custom of familiarisation. The full manning of officers and engineers would fly out to the shipyard in Japan, and stand by the new building for a month before trials. The ratings, all Singapore nationals, would join just prior to sailing.

Should the inscrutably polite Japanese desk attendants ever have watched TV's 'Big Brother', one wonders whom they would vote 'off', when a motley bunch of weary Furness Withy officers of all dimensions, ages, intellects and phobias appeared one day at the little commercial hotel in Maizuru, a small shipbuilding town in western Honshu. Big Captain Tyler right away repaired to a dim-lit cocktail bar on the top floor and ordered up warm sake, taken from a bowl. Some wandered to the restaurant where they were fed to a maximum daily allowance, after pointing out their requirements to the waitress from an array of food photos. I spent some time in my tiny room sorting out how I would fit into a diminutive bath and bed, wearing my carefully laid out blue and white kimono. In the morning, three taxis, each with a driver wearing white gloves, whisked us to the shipyard, commencing a pattern that continued unbroken for four weeks.

The Hitachi Zosen shipyard, at Maizuru, presented a clear landscape of unbroken tidiness. The day's work was about to start, and upon the open areas the work force conducted their daily limbering up. To martial music they swung their arms, and trunks, in organised calisthenics. A uniform work attire, of khaki bomber jacket and trouser, with white hardhat, added to the vision of a united workforce. We were supplied with the same, plus a boiler suit, each, when we arrived at the company manager's changing rooms. A Japanese outfitter with firm ideas about the figure of the European male had stacked a generous pile of these garments, most of them 'extra-extra large' – each would have taken three of us. A couple of bustling mama-sans, each morning, bowed us in,

'Ohio, guzimas!' they chorused, as they dipped, and, in time, we replied in kind.

Pacific Prestige, not yet fully fitted out, sat high in the water, having been launched a few days earlier. She was equipping her bridge, accommodation spaces and engine room and undergoing various surveys. To keep us busy, management suggested we take part in these. The ship was to be Hong Kong registered, and classed with the American Bureau. All safety equipment aboard H.K. registered ships closely followed the British rules. Mr.Wong, from Hong Kong, surveyed with a nervous, dedicated energy and enlisted my aid when testing the power of the air whistle.

'See! I told you! I told you!' he cried, at the end of it, after completing his own version of a test. And turning on the quizzical bunch of khaki-clad shipyard men who silently stood and stared at the excitable Chinaman, he shouted, in English,

'Turn it down, please, well down, it's far, far too noisy!'

Mr. Wong had waylaid me in one of the tween decks.

'Come with me, please,' he said, 'I want you to stand in a watchkeeping position on the bridge wing.'

Behind my back, he gave a pre-arranged signal. The men sent off a whistle blast, at which I leapt into the air. The volume was alarmingly deafening.

She completed her survey work and her exhaustive trials, in all aspects 'A1.' The shipyard gave a party with rice wine and raw unidentifiable fish, and we sailed to load grain for the U.S. West Coast, arriving there fourteen days later. A new ship is like a new car, each puff of funnel soot sent men running for brooms. *Pacific Prestige* steamed into her first port unused and immaculate. If ever a ship should blush, ours might have. She was come for her maiden load, a gift from the Orient, smelling of new paint.

Captain Tyler was a large man from Birmingham, like so many fond of his gin and duty free cigarettes, and like the rest of us pleased with his new position, yet at the same time frightened of losing it. Although our employers had not said so, we felt that we were on trial, as the majority of C.Y. Tung's seamen were native-born Chinese. Brian Tyler was no help in dispelling the gloom, as, being the senior, he felt the threat more than most. We made a circumnavigation or two, proceeding always west-about, States/Japan, Japan/Australia, Australia/Europe, Europe/States, (with a few variations in between.) We took our leaves at home, grateful that the current rules had been maintained, i.e. four months away, and two months at home, all paid, each calendar month, then returning to the same ship or a similar one. Others less fortunate would leave a ship with their payoff, not knowing when or where the next pay packet would come from, but they did not have Tung for their employer.

Two years had elapsed when a fleet message came in from London, saying, in essence, that all officers were now being offered an option. We could stay with our present employer, Furness Withy, (by this time near to becoming 'asset stripped') or move over to permanent employ with C.Y. Tung. Seminars were being held in London, at monthly intervals, in which every officer would be advised of all the pitfalls, with Management and Union officials present. There were prospects of promotion to be had, they said.

I lost no time. Within minutes my reply was winging its way by radio. I would join them, provided the last part, the important bit, of their offer stood and, of course, that matters of pay and leave remained the same.

Chapter Twelve

FILIPINO MONKEE

'Alan, you bugger, you stole my job!' Thus, over the water came the voice of Captain Brian Tyler. Two years had passed since we left the *Pacific Prestige* together, and proceeded home. I had not heard a word of him, subsequently. He had taken the redundancy option, and stayed until Furness could contain him no longer. I had fallen for the implied threats, and taken up with C.Y. Tung, but not before their hint of promotion to master had become a reality, and I had followed Brian Tyler on that same *Pacific Prestige*, into the job for which my gods had groomed me.

And now we were a pair of lonely ships passing in the night on reciprocal courses, I coming from, and Brian going to, Japan. As she approached, the disposition of her red, green and white navigation lights heralded a ship of our size, vintage and employ. Boredom and the tropical calm encircling the tip of Halmahera island had induced an hour's empty chatter on Channel 6. I was, by then, master of *Pacific Progress*, and Brian, we discovered, held a similar position on board a ship of Wheelock Marine, another Hong Kong concern. But as they say, 'different ships–different long splices', Brian was casual, whereas I was, or at least hoped to be, permanently employed.

'You've got it better than *me*, now.' Poor Brian continued to crab, 'there's no justice, Alan.'

Long ago now, it seemed, the seminars at Furness House had let fall all the arguments in a democratic way, so quaintly British. We were encouraged to make the switch to C.Y.Tung's regime, and avoid possible redundancy. For our own good, of course, and the contractual entitlements were nearly similar (but without any real Union protection.)

'But, suppose we *don't* go?' came from an awkward few. Now, all eyes stayed down. For the Company and the Merchant Navy Officers Association people well knew how much the former's balance sheets stood to lose, in redundancy payments for those who stayed.

'An offer I could not refuse,' then, resulted in a long flight to Hong Kong, a room at the Harbour Hotel in Wanchai, and, on the twenty-ninth floor of a round high-rise fortuitously named Hopewell Centre, a formal showing before my Chinese bosses. All new masters went through this initiation, and it was perhaps no bad thing, as any man is the better for well-informed advice, coming from an established source. C.Y.was absent, but I met his two deputies. Sir Y.K.Pau, a very gentle man, talked to me simply, about ships. F.S.Shih was a little harder. He was a tall, dark, well built Chinese.

'Am I boring you?' came smartly from his side of the desk, pulling me quickly out of an idle reverie, when a dissertation on the world-wide variations in the price of bunker fuel had stultified the air.

My first command, the same **Prestige**.

– Filipino Monkee –

I flew on to Sakaide, on Shikoku island, to await the *Pacific Prestige*. I could not escape the usual emotional impedimenta, more cumbrous than my baggage. Nor the feelings of euphoria at having reached the top of my profession, mingled with regret, even guilt, at displacing a regular Furness master, much more senior than I. And pride, with just getting my own ship, to have at my fingertips and handle with my brains. Nervously, I entered up the Official Log, a legal requirement when masters exchanged, in front of my dayroom guests and C.Y's staff, who watched with proud-parent smiles.

There were more than myself to deal with at the start of the Tung changeover. Our officers were from both sides, but mostly still Furness employees, which made for an uneasy mix.

We shifted ship a little way and my Chinese colleagues did not go, but stayed to watch, cluttering up my new bridge. I could not escape the many advisers, which caused me to reconsider my earlier opinions on well-informed advice. Most prominent of these was our Marine Superintendent, Captain John Ho, an energetic enthuser for the new regime, who stayed at my side throughout the short passage. He breathed confidential snippets through a cupped hand close to my ear, which he could barely reach. The piece which rang most strongly through the coming days, was at all costs to steam unswervingly past any 'boat people' without stopping. Refugees from a chaotic Vietnam were taking to frail open boats in an attempt to find an hospitable new home country. Many failed to make it and others suddenly appeared in mid-ocean, waiting to be 'rescued.' In a direct negation of international laws relating to distress at sea, I was told 'not to stop, and steam straight past.' This was not as callous as it sounded. Pirates were common in the Malacca Straits and adjacent seas. These desperate characters would ape the boat people and once close enough to throw a boarding net over a merchant ship's rail, would overcome the crew with clubs and parangs, sometimes a firearm. The safe in the master's bedroom was a prime target, Captain Ho convinced me. He also added, discomfortingly, that any vagrants such as stowaways must never be admitted on board or my management would suffer. People such as these sometimes travelled without passports and were refused entry into any country, riding on board at the owners' expense.

We lay at Hibikinada, just outside the Shimonoseki Strait, loading petcoke, strangely for England, as our ships rarely went there. The steel furnaces at Redcar burned this quality of coke. We were lucky, we happened to be suitably 'spotted.' I would be able to show off my new command to my wife. It was with added relish then, that we ridded ourselves of all visitors and at the pilot's going down I was at last, alone on my own bridge. This was a significant moment, and full of all sorts of nuances I had yet to learn about.

To my great relief we passed their favoured places and at the reefs and shallows of the Paracels, within sight of Singapore or threading through the Malacca Strait, no pirate ships were encountered. I could not but feel that I would have stopped and picked up boat people, despite Captain Ho. But half way into the Bay of Bengal, the warm wet wind of the South West monsoon began to pipe. And true to form, for he had been following my three-day position reports, from the cable/telex room at Hopewell Centre, John Ho started to compose again. Dire warnings followed, of monsoons which worsened as we progressed westward, and requests that the greatest care should be exercised. I had, as a matter of course, planned my passage according to the relevant volumes of *Ocean Routes* put out by our British Admiralty, and it was not to be faulted. Foolishly, I told him so, after which many more messages flew off the pen of Captain Ho, showing me the way.

I lacked experience in ship handling when berthing the ship in harbour, and was eager to learn. This, I believe, was the predicament of many masters. In most ports they were constrained by the bye-laws into accepting pilots and keeping a grudging watch over them. I do not consider that I ever absorbed enough knowledge, but I became adept at anchoring, on one or two occasions becoming too accomplished for my own good. My first coming to an anchor occurred at Suez. The waiting area for canal users, always full, was partitioned into small circles on the map. I was given my circle, by the Canal company. I felt my way, by weaving, oh! so slowly, between the waiting ships, going astern when I reached the spot, and yelling to the Mate, up forward,

'Let go!' The first time was easy.

With the Tung takeover things were changing fast, making way for more shipboard economies. The job of a shipmaster lost some of its mystical Godliness, while his crews became more scant. For one thing, they had taken away my Chief Steward, replacing him with a man of no consequence. That is to say, a butler of sorts, though a worthy one. On *Prestige* he was, along with the rest of the crew, Singaporean, and kept a good table, but a caterer he was not. Through all my seagoing experience, there had remained a special shipmate in the person of the Chief Steward. He would exercise budgetary control, and as a useful sideline, cajole the cook into cooperating. He was a man who could spin out the week with yesterday's left-overs and properly estimate the edibles to be re-stocked at docking. Now, I had to do it. Our feeding allowance laid down a rate of $3.50 per man per day. And it was up to me to restrain the sailors, who loved to drench their rice in anchovy essence at $12 a bottle, by locking it all away and earning the stigma of a skinflint. It was another new experience. As was the Chief Steward's sideline, the 'bond,' a treasure house of whisky, wine, liqueurs and cigarettes and a choice of beers and lagers.

This store, in a large cupboard, which I had moved from a lower deck to mine, close to my cabin door, occupied more of my time and motions than any navigational exploit or situation saving. Any discrepancies would be laid directly at my door. The preferences of all the crew had to be taken into account, because, apart from any desire to please, any goods left unsold became losses. For this reason, many brands were stocked. English engineers acquired a thirst, and beer was taken aboard 300 cases at a time. Cigarettes at $5 per carton of 200 sold very well, both American and British brands, to be consumed in the usual way and also, more difficult to assess, as a contraband form of currency, when it was concealed in unlikely places.

And, in the closing days of each month after my final visit to the bridge, I would sit over the books, balancing them into the small hours. I increased the prices by a small percentage to cover breakages and goods condemned, but this was kept a dark secret. On arrival at a port, Customs officers made a beeline for my bond, and wired up the door hasp, sealing it with a lead pellet. I learned from these people a good deal about world prices and quality, which was always attested to by the salesmen who flocked to my dayroom door bearing all sorts of 'freebies' for me to try.

Upon my promotion, I had purchased from my outfitters, Fenneck, in Plymouth, an impressive pair of shoulder epaulettes with a captain's four hefty gold stripes on a velcro strip. Ruefully, during those first months I reckoned that I should have purchased a pair of pursers' shoulder-boards in white. For, in addition to the catering and supply of the basics, I was to calculate and pay the crew wages. This did not enhance my reputation with the crew, as their balances rarely matched their expectations. Also, the accountants in Hong Kong were habitually reluctant to part with foreign deposits when I requested them, particularly when it was in the denomination of the U.S.dollar. For these, they paid a premium on the exchange. Yet crews wished to be paid in this currency, the one in which their contracts were framed. A European crew would have reacted violently, should they ever have been paid in Japanese yen, or Australian dollars. And my reputation suffered badly when I had no other cash to give my oriental crews, even though they could exchange it favourably.

'Captain, I would never have come here, if I had known.' Thus, my Indian electrician, who upon repatriation might augment his pay-off if in dollars, when he sold them on a blackish market, for his home country's rupees.

At the busy month's end, the forms covering wages and bar receipts were typed up laboriously, upon my twenty-four inch typewriter, for forwarding to the Owners at the next port. The final act in all of this was played when I opened my wall safe, taking out the rubber-banded wads of notes in three or four different currencies, and counting. If the sum did not agree with my account's bottom line a troublesome few days would ensue. If it did I would remove a bottle of scotch from my meagre bar profits and celebrate my success, a dangerous dip into hedonism from which shipmasters would do well to abstain.

My initial voyage, ended on England's north-east coast on a pleasant note as Judy came up to Immingham to spend a few days on board. The 'butler' produced a fresh menu with newly purchased supplies. We sat at my round saloon table with its huge rotating Party Susan, put there for a Chinese crew – should we ever be equipped with one – to support the many additions they loaded onto it with which to season their rice.

We sailed from England without any heroic farewells, as our Hong Kong flag put us down as denizens of the East unlikely to be missed. We followed the trade route of most Panamax bulk carriers of the period. This was westward, to the U.S. East coast to load for Japan via Panama, either coal from Hampton Roads or grain from the Mississippi. The Atlantic crossing, most people agreed should be made well to the south, thus avoiding the areas of storms, seasonal icebergs and adverse current in the form of the Gulf Stream. Not many would attempt the Great Circle route to the north, which, though shorter, would run close to the risky Grand Banks of Newfoundland.

In the north Pacific, a quite different set of rules apply. The Pacific, in spite of its name, is a big brother to the Atlantic, the violence of its seas a good deal more manly. By the side of its shelving depths, in an eyrie not far from San Francisco, a collective of Weather Routeing wizards cook up their hocus-pocus. Or so it seemed to me.

Weather routeing had always existed historically, in one form or another. But with the advent of our modern breed of ocean tramp, the science had gained a new, fashionable acceptance like colonic irrigation or marathon runs. Sophisticated new recording instruments plotted the path of storms. For a fee that the shipowner (for once, naïve) found attractive, the weather-routeing services would purport to find, for all of the community of captains, their calmest way across the oceans. This, of course, would ensure the ship's earliest arrival, the least expenditure upon fuel for the distance run, and a minimal amount of heavy weather hull damage. But, in my experience, these felicitous circumstances rarely happened. I had once chosen a route (when not weather routed) through the Hawaian group, well to the south, and not much longer, in which I had found my own good weather all the way. The routers often lost the plot half way across, when fickle weather systems played pranks. But, worst of all, with a judgement based on serendipity, they under-estimated the effects of the winds. For the bluff bowed, deeply wallowing bulk carrier any moderate headwind with its attendant swell will sharply reduce the effect of the propellor and the ship's speed through the water. The ship will slip further and further back in their mural displays, until it becomes too late to revise any routeing instruction.

As far as Long Beach, our bunker port, we were safe, securely removed from their advices. But then came the continuation to Yokohama. Through the Unimak Pass they sent us, and north of the Aleutian chain, into the chill mists, with no turning back. Moderate gales from ahead stayed with us, prolonging the passage all the way.

Japan then led the world in mechanised cargo handling at new ports hugely landscaped with concrete, some with artificial islands. The discharge of any bulk was achieved in one or two days. This imposed the maximum stress on the captain and crew, for after a sea passage of four to six weeks there were many projected tasks to be completed, only possible when alongside, so leading to 'skimping.' Meanwhile, we waited impatiently, for news of our next employment. Even the charterers were caught by surprise on occasion. An exchange of telex took place,

'Please advise our next voyage instructions and destination, regards, Master.'

'Next voyage prospects not yet known. Please proceed according to your own discretion, regards. '

I headed, slowly, for Australia, and always afterwards, did the same, without asking.

Sometimes, the Japanese shipbrokers, with inexpert English, were distracted by considerations of commercial rivalry. One of my sailing messages began,

'Dear Captain, you must please read this message with eyes closed.'

Pacific Prestige now did proceed to Australia, to Geelong, where we would load more wheat for Antwerp. The shippers wished to avoid the Suez Canal. If in no great hurry for the cargo, why pay canal dues? The alternative sea passage was one of the longest possible, in the day to day steaming of a merchantman.

Australia, when passing below the huge gulf they have christened the Australian Bight, appears so big as to be a continent in itself, as of course, it is. The weather there is often boisterous and always the seas are heavy with a high swell rolling up unbroken, from the Antarctic. So that, after five or six days, when Cape Leuwin is reached, a whole voyage, it seems, has taken place. But no. There is still the limitless expanse of Indian ocean to cross until the cape of Africa is sighted, and none too closely, either, for this is an area of 'freak' waves big enough to break your ship's back. We are not yet there, by a long chalk. Once round Point Aghulas we turn north-west, then north and steam through a year's seasons, crossing the doldrums to the equator and on into more homely yet just as treacherous seas, from West Africa to the Bay and English Channel. Our lonely horizons end here, suddenly with an alarming excess of strange craft steaming in every direction.

The voyage to Antwerp lasted forty four days, a lengthy tedium, yet frightening enough to contemplate before we put our nose out of the harbour on sailing day. I had approached the charterer, for permission to stop the ship off Cape Town, where by my pre-arrangement, ship's mail could have been forwarded and a boat load of fresh produce could await us. The message was bounced excitedly to the Owners in Hong Kong, who despatched to me, with some asperity, a negative reply,

'... on no account,' etc.,etc. It would have involved a 'deviation', with the cost of our daily hire pro-rata'd to the Owner, from the charterer.

On arrival at Antwerp, my six-month period of duty on *Prestige* was over. I proceeded home to the usual warm welcome from my wife. My girls were more guarded. The teenagers knew that for a foreseeable time they would come second, an unavoidable hazard in the strange life of their seafarer Daddy. Three months now, and we would spend a good leave together. For those three months I would be paid. But, unlike Furness Withy days, my pay stopped there, until I put to sea again.

Mr. Wong, in charge of Sea Personnel, had put me in some kind of slot, and when some years later I asked him why, he said that out of the two of his ships manned by Chinese and of which ex-Furness men would now sail as master, the *Pacific Progress* was put there especially for me. His judgement was premature. However, I was not to know that then, and looked forward to a return to the old traditions, with Chinese seamen who were said to be polite and biddable.

The two ships, *Pacific Progress* and *Asian Progress*, were on time charter to a New York concern, though still engaged on the well travelled routes of world–wide bulk trading. Likewise, my mode of joining was no different, that is, an economy flight with Cathy Pacific direct to Hong Kong, the heart-stopping touch-down with our wingtips slicing, it seemed, through the tenements' clothes lines of drying laundry. Thence a visit to Hopewell Centre before the short hop to the ship, lying in Japan. This was no initiation, as they all knew me now. More a matter of having me on a short string, prepared for a quick dash to a brief ship stop-over.

The big coincidence, then, was complete and unexpected. My visiting day at Hopewell Centre happened to match that of the Furness Withy Managing Director, there, I had to assume, on some pretty high level stuff concerning the joint operation of our two companies. A sumptuous Chinese lunch had been laid on to foster the *entente cordial*. I was invited, and seated at a round table for eight, next to the M.D. We shared an exclusiveness as, despite the helpful attentions of our Chinese hosts who told us what we were eating, we could not hide our astonishment at the endless procession of mysterious delicacies. Brightly coloured and strangely tasting, we made fools of ourselves pushing the food around our plates with unmanageable chopsticks. The M.D. had an expressive face, and I looked for an echo as my teeth sunk into a fishy tasting morsel coated with a bitter chocolate. However, our common origins led to sympathetic and unpretentious conversation.

Filipino Monkee

The whole government of Queensland, it seemed, was there.

Quite naturally, the dialogue concerned the new crew arrangements then existing.

'And what do you think of it all, now, Captain Jones?' the M.D. said, 'would you like to have the white crews back again?'

I believed that this was not a leading question, and also that I answered it honestly, and without any secondary motive.

'I must say, Sir, we don't seem to have the same old union trouble in the way that we did,' I replied.

The M.D's face darkened with, I was sure, bitter recollection. In Britain, the National Union of Seamen had not long resumed work following an emasculating strike, which had no basis in any real disagreement. The British fleet tied up, as each ship arrived home. In addition, our own officer's association was claiming unreasonable pay hikes which even I thought reckless and stupid.

The M.D.'s features tightened.

'No,' he said, 'I'm very sure you wont be getting any more of *that*.'

This was a man who could not alter the economics of shipping commerce nor the flow of commodities world wide, but he was at the seat of power when it came to the method, the operation of ships. And this brief exchange at the Chinese lunch, remains, to me, most significant, for it preceded the 're-flagging' of many of our ships and the extensive employment of foreign crews.

New houses built in rows quickly lose their sameness, and Tung's modern fleet of standard design changed in the same way, each ship growing its own patina from the style of the people who lived in it. Identical to the *Prestige* in size and layout, *Pacific Progress* had acquired an air of its own, even extending to smells, as I quickly appreciated, after hauling myself up her gangway. The smell was of Chinese cooking, of sesame oil with a little ghee butter. But happily, it turned out, on board this ship I had a Chief Steward, one of the old school who took to me, because, to him, I was also one of those. Tam, a mannerly man from Macao, saw to it that one English menu was provided each day, for the four non-Chinese – myself, one engineer from the Tyne, an English third mate and George, my Indian Chief Engineer from Kerala. Other meals were conducted in the Chinese way, with a main dish in the table centre being consumed communally, by all seated there, with chopsticks. On the sideboard there steamed a large slow cooker of rice, from which, jumping up at intervals, they replenished their bowls generously. But standards of cleanliness were sadly absent, and I revived the British custom of Master's weekly inspections of accommodation, galley and storerooms. To the crew, this innovation aroused a lot of excited curiosity.

'What is he doing, going through our cabins? What does he plan to get out of it?' they asked one another.

The cook, far from disgruntled, flung open his frozen meat room door with a huge grin.

'Po'! Bi'!,' he repeated, gesturing in a way which suggested mental problems of a sort.

I turned to Adam, the mate,

'Tell him,' I said, 'I know full well it is pork and beef, I just want to see that it is still fresh, and good.'

We were fixed for a cargo of coal at Gladstone, in Queensland. It was the first order ever of Australian coal to be consigned to Italy. This event triggered an official inspection tour of the ship by the Australian Minister of Mines, and his *entourage*, followed by speeches and a slap-up lunch ashore. I was informed that the cargo was split for delivery in two parts, at La Spezia and Venice. At the mention of the latter place, an opportunity presented itself. One of the 'perks' of the job allowed me to take my wife with me. She would love Venice, followed by a month or two's cruising. I immediately put in my request, to the management.

More conveniently north-about the great continent, we passed inside the Barrier Reef and through the Torres Strait, to the canal at Suez.

And there, again, still touching upon the raw, the eternal spirit of the Egyptian *backsheesh*. The boatloads of Suez Company inspectors, Customs, Quarantine and Immigration officials with their several assistants had grown, along with their demands. Unhappily, due to no fault of my own, my supply of 'presents' had dwindled, and the stage for a sullen protest was speedily set. While at Gladstone, where the market was good, I had placed a large order for 'Marlboro' cigarettes. The supplier had been unable to fill it, being unprepared for such a sizeable demand. With crew consumption as high as ever, we were now in short supply.

'That's all I can manage today, I'm afraid,' I confessed before them all. I was compelled to limit each official to one carton of 200. This they saw as an attempt at levelling, insulting by not compensating higher ranks with a larger share.

'But Captain ...' hunched, with brown hands held palms uppermost, 'this is not acceptable – never, never before have we been treated in this way!'

Displays of histrionics filled my room until the boats could wait no longer. They were offered bottles of spirit, as an alternative, but to the teetotal Arab, this was not much appreciated. After more pleadings and imprecations, however, they dragged themselves away, seeing that in my bond there was so little left. (I did have the foresight, before arrival, to conceal my reserves, in another place.) But I had not considered the Suez Canal Pilot, who would board when our turn for transit came up.

We lay for the night to an anchor, awaiting the arrival of this personage, who came with the dawn, trailing a miasma of diesel smoke from a sputtering launch and a sigh of garlic as a pasty-skinned Egyptian in snowy tropical whites shouldered his way through my wheelhouse door.

There was a time when Canal pilots ranked with God, as their companies, having connected every ocean, inclined to the distinctly divine. The British empire builders, during their country's shipping dominance, had nurtured a primacy for their pilots at Suez, and though the posts were shared by the French and others, the British had, until Abdul Nasser sequestered their jobs, ruled with an autocratic hand. At their ignominious departure a cry went up from their representative body claiming that there were no pilots capable of replacing them. This turned out to be false, and within a short time others had taken over. The Russians were there, Poles and Germans and, of course, local Egyptian master mariners, all doing well. Yet the slur had been made. Everybody felt its keen embrace.

The anchor was weighing. Formalities were quickly made, with hands shaken.

'Good morning, Captain, right-handed propeller?'

'How are you, Pilot? Yes, right handed, and the main engines are diesel.'

He shaped a course for the canal entrance, a patch of emerald wedged between shoulders of umber sand. A quiet, orderly bridge.

'Captain, do you think you might have forgotten ... something?'

Oh, no! It could not be, pilots just didn't ask. It was beneath them.

'Sorry, pilot, what is that?'

'Captain – you know – I would appreciate one carton, please, I prefer Marlboro'.'

Never! They had all gone. I'd dished out enough. What kind of a fool did he take me for?

'I'm afraid not, pilot. I've given out all I have to all the other ... people. Next trip, maybe, ha! ha!.' A restless twitch of anger, at my side. A voice slightly raised.

'Captain, you are going to – *I* don't know where you are going – but you do not tell me that you have no cigarettes?'

'I most certainly do, pilot. I only have just enough.'

'Captain, I insist.'

Say no more. What can he do?

'No!'

A gesture of frustration, impatience.

'Then, Captain, I will not conn your ship. You can do it yourself.'

My wife came with me.

– Filipino Monkee –

With a lazy turn of the head, he looked the steersman in the eye, and motioned with his index finger to the left. This is a standard international signal, well understood, and means 'to put the rudder to the left.' He did. The bow headed for the shore.

'See ... she's headed for the bank, Captain.'

For sure, the small town of Port Tewfik, a block of white squares perched on the left bank, lay sleeping a few yards away. Even at that hour an open gharry stood on the tarmac road leading to Port Said, awaiting a fare. I could smell the hot dung of its ponies, the farm life close by.

Turning to the wheel, I shouted, 'Check her!' But the steersman was confused by the chain of counter commands.

The pilot, cool from knowing his limits of danger more closely than I, stood as a silent screwball, playing Russian roulette with me.

In that fraction of a second, while the bow swung from side to side of the canal, I might have been a young mother with her baby in direst danger. Desperate decisions were called for. I could have easily managed the conn – it was a simple matter of steering between small buoy markers, but illegal, by those strange mid-eastern laws, for me to try. We had the whole canal yet to do, with all its officialdom. But, at all costs, the confusion must be contained.

I capitulated.

'O.K., pilot, O.K.,O.K., I'll get you the damned cigarettes.'

Handing the bond keys to the watch officer, I requested that he remove three cartons, holding back two, for the pilot changes to come, at Ismailia, and Port Said to sea.

This last gave me short shrift and pleaded to leave early, departing at the first buoy, and leaving me to negotiate the long sea channel, un-piloted and illegal. I welcomed the escape, and hurried away at full speed from that mischievous, madcap Middle East.

* * *

'What's this place like, then?'

The challenge of seamen everywhere was on the lips of the *Progress'* crew as we passed up the Tyrrhenian Sea, to the port of La Spezia. They would find out their own way. Useless to point out that a short bus ride away lay relics of Rome and the beauty of renaissance Florence, they had been at sea far too long. They would seek out their cosy bars, with chemical beer and unreachable girls, and gaudy shops strung up with T-shirts and souvenirs, then wander back on board with a sailors' *'je ne sais quoi'* , a spirit of dull tedium, wishing themselves back in more cordial territory with someone they knew well.

'Not much to this dump, is there?' they would say, turning their eyes to sea again.

Good fortune found a better estate for me, as Judy Gray was waiting in the Agents' office. She had buttoned up her courage and flown down that day to Genoa, coming aboard with the entry officials. But, as ship wives often find, there were longish times when she had to sit by herself.

Adam, my deputy, was chief officer of the *Progress*. The name was self-given, a temporary handle more easily suited to English-speaking ships than the difficult Chinese sounds imposed at his birth. But Adam was pure Chinese – Hong Kong Chinese – a dark, good looking boy, steady and married, with above average intelligence moderated by a dull British education. This had instilled in him ideas of consideration for the underdog, along with many other instincts utterly un-Chinese. It ignored the implacable racism that churns in a chinaman's breast, easily as much as it does in his western contemporary's. Helping to 'stir the pot' within Adam, was the continuing British rule in Hong Kong, completely out of order as far as he was concerned. And Adam wanted my job, which he saw as an Anglified sinecure. The last obstruction to getting it was me. So there we were, I, with my own prejudices, and Adam, inwardly grown like the trunk of a palm, each overlaying new leaf now drying fibrous, obscuring its earlier, more artless folds.

In the harbour at La Spezia, local ship chandlers, hungry as wolves, pitched into the ship with their price-lists. Food with the Chinese ranked high in their existence and these people knew it well. Also, my crew's spending habits were highly developed, they knew what they wanted and were prepared to pay, much more so than their British counterparts. Many items were unobtainable, such as chinese cabbage out of season, condiments and sauces intrinsically chinese. Thus, the chandler who could persuade and promote his produce, not to mention his honesty, would prevail. Every wile in the book was needed for this feat, as there was both myself and my crew to coax.

It was narrowed down, as the weaker ones faded away, to two, who offered the most. One, a clear-cut shyster, the other having a look of washed-out integrity. It mattered little, payment would come only after each item was checked and weighed. I chose the latter, the choice was unavoidably mine. Adam preferred the former, who had promised him Chinese delights.

'Why, sir? *Why* did you take *him*?' Thus, a little later, snapped Adam, his olive eyes black with suspicion, anger and dislike. The rest lay fallow and unspoken, but long remembered. I had, for certain, taken the captains' backhander. I had cheated the Chinese, just as all captains did.

I swelled with pride when I showed Judy Gray my bridge in its working prime, gazing through the forward windows at a distant bow lifting impressively to the swell

'Board of Trade sports' on Fridays at 4.30.

and down onto the black topsides of her, polished wetly by the waves. We sailed down and through the narrow Straits of Messina, meeting on the way Scylla and Charybdis, the clashing rock and upwelling whirlpool that had frightened the ancients, then up a sludgy Adriatic, to Venice. Heavy industry with its coal and power sources and our berth, lay in the Malamocco channel, keeping us away from the city. But a days' french leave was taken, despite Adam's troubles, and Chief Engineer George's likewise, while we headed for Saint Mark's Square, the Bridge of Sighs, and points beyond.

Our cruise continued, the next cargo waiting at Port Kamsar near Conakry, a load of African bauxite for the Alcoa aluminum company at Point Comfort, Texas. She saw the Russian fish factory ships depleting the ocean of small fry off Nouadhibou, and was the source of African boys' collective delight in shinning up bare trees behind the port to drop green coconuts at her feet.

With half of the Atlantic crossed, the Dragon Boat festival day demanded a Chinese banquet. Tam excelled in providing it and produced a menu in English that he typed, with startling translations into English onto a memo pad.

About this time, poor George, my little Chief from Trivandrum, showed signs of strain. It had become a custom for my wife to sit with him as an adjunct to meals, and settle him with her small talk. But George, with escalating tales of a young and beautiful wife in India, and an improbable slice of shares in the Bombay Taj Mahal Hotel, had scanned the colour prints of my daughters. He decided that he would marry the middle one. The first signs of a breakdown were beginning to show.

Yet these domestic problems melted away when the time came to change cargoes. And all the more so when it was from dirty to clean. The bauxite residues lay heaped in corners when the Alcoa bulldozers had finished, and piled along deckhead beams too high for ladders to reach. We were booked to load a full cargo of corn at New Orleans, for Rotterdam. Corn was a 'capacity full' load, it reached parts of the hold other cargoes never did. A thorough high-pressure hose wash-down and subsequent drying must be performed upon our seven large holds, at nothing less than eight hours per hold. But the steaming time between Point Comfort, and a berth somewhere up the Mississippi clocked up no more than three days. Upon arrival, I was obliged to tender my notice of readiness, 'ship ready in all respects to load.' If I did not, the ship would go 'off hire', a condition unacceptable to the Owner. I scanned the charter party for escape clauses, such as SHEX, (Sundays and Holidays Excepted) but found none. I would dawdle as much as I dared. We would do our best.

'We must be ready, Adam,' I said.

Eastern sailors are small in stature. They wrestle with the backlashing hoses, become weary at the tubs of sweepings totalling tons, hoisted forty feet by rope from the floor of the hold to the deck and dumped into the sea. We split the *Progress* crew into two shifts working day and night, even the cook and his galley staff, with the engine room men called out to help.

And the hurricane season had started. A full-out hold washing requires cargo hatches open to the sky, with the covers rolled back. This act, of course, renders the ship unseaworthy, as any seas whipped up by a wind would crash down into the cargo spaces, quickly capsizing her. But there was no other way in which we could be ready, so we kept a weather eye, and hoped.

On the third day, with holds clean and only a little damp, we sent our ropes ashore at a deep-water grain berth, just above the Huey Long bridge in outer New Orleans. There was, though, the gauntlet of the Grain Inspectors still to be run. This lesser breed of ruffians (for that is how the seafarer saw him) swept aboard in their numbers, equipped with bug-finders and powerful flashlights. Within an hour we had 'failed inspection.'

The justice of that decision was open to doubt. Some said that the tall standing silos which now threw their long shadows over us, were half empty, and still awaited two or three of the hundred boxcar freight trains which made their way down from the prairies. To fail inspection came in as a useful artifice to switch the blame. Some said that I did not subscribe sufficient beer to ease the gentlemen's burden. In any case we went 'off-hire' for a day and a half, spent fine sweeping, while the disapproval of a distant Captain John Ho was generally felt, with that well-remembered acid look of his hanging in the mind's eye.

Judy and I grasped the opportunity, as we lay within a tolerable cab-fare of downtown and old Bourbon Street. The day coincided with our twenty-fifth wedding anniversary. I took my bride ashore. We visited a *bijoutier,* in a state where stones are cheap, and purchased a large aquamarine. And later, we took George with us to Mister T's, for the largest beefsteak he had ever seen.

Oversize vessels such as the *Progress* were a common sight on the Mississippi river, whose milk-brown waters flow adequately full, wide and deep from Baton Rouge to the sea, a good two days' steaming. But at its mouth the river silts. We could sink the ship to a draft of forty feet, plus or minus a couple of inches but not to be exceeded, this being the river's depth at the point of its spilling into the Gulf of Mexico.

'We must lift the maximum load,' I had said to Adam.

Gingerly, we passed outward, with the best of the mud pilots on my bridge, he who knew where the shallower patches were. She 'sniffed the bottom' once, with a 'veering off' or two, away from the rudder's influence.

Once clear of the Florida Strait we turned to the north-east, with the full strength of the Gulf Stream behind us.

'Just to liven up the weekend,' the men would say. Regularly on Friday afternoons at four-thirty, a muster drill at Boat and Fire Stations was called. 'Board of Trade Sports', they named it, an overpowering nuisance where everybody got rigged in his lifejacket and wound out a lifeboat or two. But they all knew that one day it might be for real, and attended as the law demanded.

'Shall I send the book around?' The coded question was put to me by the watch officer in the morning. This was our little order book informing department heads that the drill was to take place, and demanding their acknowledging 'moniker'. Everyone had signed.

Except George. The chief had been behaving strangely since we cleared the Florida panhandle and broke out into the Atlantic. He had always dressed neatly, usually a Nehru style jacket and trousers in the Indian yellowish khaki. But now, bare chested, he sported nothing but a sarong and sandals. He played his tapes of Kerala style country music at full volume, and forgot meal times.

The intercom phone on my desk gave a small ring.

'I am sorry, Captain,' came George's rounded Indian accents, 'I am too busy to attend the boat drill, today.'

'Now, come on, George, if we let you off, everyone will want off!' I said.

'I am sorry Captain. No.'

'Now look here, George ...'

'NO!' We did not see him, at all, that day.

During that autumn the North Atlantic was in a wall-to-wall calm, and through days and nights we made good speed, it seemed that nothing could stop us. So that shock and amazement pulled us all out of deep and innocent sleep, at about 3 o'clock of a still morning. A deathly, dark-dense quiet. The engines had stopped. The ship lay scarcely moving, creaking gently. Then, breaking out all at once, strident urgency noises. Every buzzer, auto-alarm and bell announced its walk-on part. Red and amber lights flashed in the alleyways, on the bridge, beside my bed. The gyro compass, the radar, all radio transmitters including S.O.S. – OFF. Every light, including the emergency navigation lights – OFF. No other ship could see us or hear us. The Duty Engineer and the Officer of the Watch ran frantically from spot to spot, searching, finding no fire, no collision, nothing under water. Looking to the emergency batteries – QUICK!

Then, down below, they found George, not smiling, but palely satisfied.

'Now, that was a real drill, a *real* emergency,' he boasted, 'I *told* him I was too busy.'

George had gone below in the night, had disabled the emergency generator and 'shut down the job.'

I worded as discreet a cable to Hong Kong as my lack of doctor knowledge would allow. *The Shipmasters Medical Guide*, my bible on such occasions, diagnosed mental breakdown. I suspected it would be the end of the road for George professionally, but there was no alternative. I requested that they relieve him on arrival at Rotterdam. I informed the Second Engineer that he must now act as 'Chief', but not to tell George.

Judy Gray also, went home from Rotterdam. My stay on board had not long to run, and it was a most convenient point from which to send her, she might have been stuck in Japan.

'Why are you sending your wife home?' Louis Wong demanded. He had flown in from Hong Kong, not for us specifically, but due to unexpected developments, he would 'investigate.'

'Chief Engineers, you know, are hard to replace. Much harder,' he announced, carefully watching my face, 'than Masters.'

He had stopped first at the cabins of the Chinese officers and then came up to mine. I did not care for his methods.

'In the end, the Master is always responsible.' The well-worn adage ran, yet again, through my mind.

– Filipino Monkee –

Our new chief was an excellent fellow from the Blue Funnel line, and within a short time we were firm friends. One more brief trip, another bauxite load, and my turn came up for relief.

Nothing Louis Wong had fashioned from his vision of future *Pacific* and *Asian Progresses* was ever revealed, and my association with them now ceased. He kept his cards close to his chest. It was left to the London extension of his department to find a new berth for me. It was a big one. They did not, out of C.Y's stable at least, come any bigger.

The *Pacific Courage*, with 120,000 tonnes deadweight carrying capacity, was nearly twice the size of the Panamaxes, and of a class suitably christened 'Cape'. Too wide for the canals at Suez or Panama, she was banished like some mythical ship of the Argonauts, to making her long hauls round the 'Capes.'

She was built in Korea with an 'optional extra' putting her into a higher insurance class. Internal strengthening, with thicker plates at the bow, stern and rudder entrance had fortified her for navigating in surface sea ice. Which was just as well, for we saw a lot of it. She was on a long-term time charter to the British Steel Corporation. Her main function was to feed their furnaces, at Port Talbot, Redcar or Hunterston with the raw iron ore, which came in pea-shaped pellets from Port Cartier. This Canadian export terminal was situated some way down the frequently frozen St.Lawrence River.

There the sea ice comes in many forms. Some melts and is re-frozen, presenting a lumpy terrain. The new-season ice grows only down, deepening each winter month to an impassable two metres thick on occasions. My introduction to the brash sea ice at the start of the season, commenced with an ear-crashing clangour. We knew the edge of the ice was there, meandering across the chart from Cape Breton Island to the coast of Labrador, and we had suitably reduced speed for our initial contact. Even so, with an empty ship already echoing like a bell-tower, the cavernous hold spaces amplified the new sounds of ice shards piling, cart-wheeling and jostling down the ship's side.

Later in the season, the ice took on a more damaging pose. Nearly a metre thick, it slowed *Pacific Courage,* bravely shuddering, to a halt. It was time to put her strengthened bow and stern to the test. The tried method, they told me, was to put the engines ahead at full speed, stop, then come full astern. Then, like a powered ram, charge full speed ahead again; repeating the process, until by a stroke of luck you battered your way into an open 'lead.' It didn't work. Our engine power was sadly inadequate. After a number of attempts, we had moved ahead a bare twenty feet. We were well and truly 'fast.' Darkness came down, and we were all alone. But I had seen earlier in the day, passing upon her lawful occasion in the distance, the brilliant magenta coloured hull of a Canadian Coast Guard icebreaker. We called her on the radio. I was told to address my request to the Coast Guard H.Q., in Halifax, Nova Scotia. At dawn, the icebreaker

John A. Macdonald came up, circled round us, and with her enormous engine power, cracked open the grubby white mass. We followed, like good King Wenceslas' page, in her pooling wake, until new leads took us into clear water.

'I must not anchor in the ice.' I told myself this, repeatedly, lest I forget. The ice could freeze around us, and should it drift in a mass would take us with it, leaving a length of my chain and one good stockless anchor behind, deep in the obsidian ooze. So we stopped and drifted, a condition not conducive to sleep for ship keepers in shoaling water.

The summer months brought a brief lease of the sea's countenance, in the shapes of crystalline blue icebergs, bergy bits and growlers. To see and avoid striking them, (as it is a safer prospect to sail through a visible herd than chance upon a maverick drifter, in mid-ocean) I chose my summertime route through the Belle Isle Strait, between Labrador and the island of Newfoundland. At its northerly entrance the sea lies bejewelled with bergs in many sizes and shapes, an awesome and most beautiful sight. Sea fog adds to the difficulty of navigation in this region. When beset by a mix of dense fog and numerous bergs, I would stop the ship at night, and continue slow steaming during the day, with as many extra pairs of eyes at my side as I could muster. A radar scanner will not detect the growlers and smaller bergs, which could have easily punctured the vessel's hull.

The whole expanse of the North Atlantic was sometimes fog-bound. This is the hardest condition for the shipmaster, for it requires his presence night and day upon the bridge, until it 'clears up.' One wishes for the more routine storm, and is not long in getting it. A staunch ship will survive these, but not without an extra share of wear and tear. At four years old, the *Courage* showed corrosion and small fractures of her steel fabric below decks. The random concentration of heavy weights, such as iron ore in bulk, places an unusual strain upon the longitudinal strength. A ship's hull built to meet such usage will not last many years.

Severe gales and high seas are the standard fare of Atlantic crossings. *Pacific Courage* would take them in her stride when loaded and bound homeward to the United Kingdom. An eastbound heading put the usual weather all behind her, her weight made her nearly immovable and the seas washed, more or less harmlessly, over her decks. Steaming west to Port Cartier for another load presented a different picture altogether. For then she was 'flying light' with no weight in her besides one hold and bottom tanks full of water ballast, and the gales, nearly always westerly, were from ahead. On these occasions she tossed and plunged, kicking up her heels like an angry bullock at a rodeo show, her bows rising and then coming down to land slamming and noisily vibrating upon the sea's torn surface in a widespread layer of foam. The further north our route took us, the worse it became. The English Channel, as an entrance and exit to the ocean, was the one I always chose, in preference to 'north about' Scotland, whenever we were bound for the U.K's eastern coast.

Cold and stormy weather, to my constant surprise, never bothered the Filipinos. These happy, tough brown people made up the crew of the *Courage*. The mix of Filipino ratings with British officers had been identified by our watchful Management as an ideal one, and all the ships were eventually so manned, after trying out seamen from Singapore, Hong Kong, India and Bangladesh. Large numbers of Filipinos were leaving their land to become servants and labourers in all parts of the world due to hardships at home. Our sailors came both from the island jungle villages and the impoverished parts of suburban Manila, where their Union had set up a workable arrangement with our people in Hong Kong. Anyone could see that they were all of the Roman faith, for they adorned their cabin bulkheads with religious icons, framed pictures of the Madonna (next to their sisters) and colourful wall hangings of the crucifixion. Common beliefs made them a group working to the same end, and so far as making a fine crew was concerned they were the best we could have wished for. They braved the sub-zero climate more stoutly than a Caucasian might have done, and lived in their survival suits. These suits were expensive, and after a change of crew during which the suits disappeared for all time into home-bound kit-bags, our management insisted we collect them up and sign them out each time temperatures plummeted.

No one is perfect. In one area of duty, the Filipino disgraced his calling. Throughout all those long, stormy passages we kept one of them up there on the bridge. His proper duty was as a lookout, though with all the flying spume impinging upon his eyeballs and the stygian winter's dark, it is unlikely that he would have seen much. By his side, the VHF radio crackled and spilled out a distant unrecognisable babble. Two far-off Spanish trawlermen speaking to one another, perhaps, or the buzz of twice bounding waves from radios a thousand miles away. The radio-phone was left, switched on, for one reason – distress. It remained on Channel 16, the international distress frequency on which all ships listened and broadcast, should they ever be unlucky enough to need to do so. A frequency for this purpose only, and kept clear by all seamen, in a holy understanding of all that was good.

But the happy-go-lucky Filipino, with an irreligious shedding of 'all that stuff,' played with the phone, lifting it from its hook when the watch officer was out of earshot and speaking silly talk into it, transmitting for a hundred miles what was the Filipino challenge of the day.

'Filipino *monkee*!' he would sing in a two-note chime. Very soon the air would become live, the very air held most sacrosanct for distress. All round us other ships, each with their Filipino standing by their phone, would answer, in duty bound,

'Fililpino *mon*kee!' they all sang. And followed it up with Donald Duck noises, a howling hyena, raspberries in plenty, and mild abuse in their own language.

'Just a silly fad,' we said. But some time later, when it spread too far to be ignored, far enough to dominate all the oceans, we took measures to stop it. Any legitimate distress message just did not stand a chance.

It was not often we were sent to Poland. The miners' strike had depleted most of the steel producers' stockpiles, and we were sent far afield for new supplies. A cargo of coal lay at Gdansk. We were despatched for a partial load only, as all routes out of the Baltic were too shallow for our loaded draft. The Harbour Master, an important figure in this major port, came off to guide the big ship to her berth. We were honoured to have so important a personage. But he sat far too long in my dayroom when the time came to go home.

'Captain,' he said, 'do you think I could have some coffee, and if you have any ham ...? I will send to your home a most beautiful present!'

In Poland, a country at peace, they stood in line every day for food. The children stood first, with their place relieved by the mother, and after half a day father took over. With one day's queueing, they might end up with a loaf, whether a senior harbour master or not.

We returned to South Wales, a land of much greater abundance, to striking miners. They had taken over the high gantry cranes, and hurled missiles – stones and bolts and nuts – down at us as we docked, for in their eyes we were a blacklegging ship.

Harbour pilots there in the Swansea area, appeared as tolerably normal creatures. I had by now learned my anchor drill. Skill was not required in the dropping, but for positioning the ship in the right place. The Swansea pilots, because there were some who did not ever learn, came aboard to anchor the ships themselves. The *Courage* was a big heavy ship to anchor, and a lot of cable was run out.

'You'll be alright here, Skip,' the pilot had assured me 'real good holding ground, here.'

During the night, an Atlantic depression came scorching up the Bristol Channel, and stretched the cable some more. When a ship drags its anchor, the vibrations are felt throughout the structure. I was awakened by these, and moved quickly to the bridge where the officer on anchor watch 'had not noticed.' Ships on either side of us stood still. We slid slowly back towards the foreshore, and were much closer now, but at that moment one of the others started to drag down onto us. It was our standard precaution to keep the engines 'warmed through' and I thanked the Almighty, not for the first time, that this was so. With the south-westerly shrieking, we heaved up as quickly as the wind would allow and removed ourselves from the port. I steamed down to Lundy

Island, where there was a precarious lee, working back to Swansea later, when the calm came.

Our regular pilot boarded, for a 'second attempt.'

'The holding ground's quite firm in that spot, Captain, no one ever dragged from there,' he grumbled, shaking his head.

We had formed firm friendships with these men and the crew of the Swansea pilot boat who brought out our mail to the anchorage. When my turn came for relief, the pilots offered to take me in their boat across the water to my home in North Devon, provided I laid on the lunch.

This, unhappily, never happened. The boat was taken away for a service on that very day.

I was 'bounced' from one *Pacific* to another, covering the same ground, more or less, as before. My favourite of all was *Pacific Pride*, her funnel seemed a mite taller, her plastic dark wood veneers a more handsome oak, or perhaps, with a name like that, she deserved a little sympathy, when she innocently came before a fall. But that was later on.

Injustice I could never abide, and considered my crew to be my own charges. A Filipino cook named Marcos had completed his contract, which was for one year, and requested relief. A short time later we stopped at Manila, an ideal place to change the cooks I believed, and called for his replacement. Hong Kong could find no one, and, more importantly, did not respond.

Marcos was very angry. Galley meals deteriorated.

We steamed on, for Australia. I requested again, adding that Marcos showed a good deal of strain and this was bad for morale. Would they please relieve him in Australia?

'No,' said Hong Kong, 'immigration department difficulties did not permit such a transfer of aliens within the territory.' No one believed this.

Marcos now very, very angry. When he wielded his long knives, people stood clear. Now, I too, became angry. I composed a telegram to the seamens' union in Manila, asking them to intercede. They copied my message to Hong Kong.

No relief appeared in Australia, nor yet any word of one. We all knew how long the next leg would be, to Europe maybe. Marcos became distracted. I cabled again, to ask them 'why?'

The reply from Hong Kong commenced with: 'Understand you contacted seamens' union in Manila ref. cook Marcos ...' There followed a few lines of rebuke, that I should dare to do such a thing. Marcos had to wait until Rotterdam, two months overdue.

A little later, a Filipino donkeyman received news of a family member's death, and was overtaken by a form of grief under which he had lost control, becoming violent towards his shipmates. I knew, now, that nothing was more certain than that he would not be repatriated, as we lay in Richards Bay, South Africa, a coal terminal remote from all other life, with air fares prohibitive. And it was shortly after the Marcos incident.

In Richards Bay the 'Flying Angel' kept a small mission. I called upon the young Chaplain, an ordained English priest. This gentleman came aboard, and shut himself away with the donkeyman. He was successful in calming the man. Full of gratitude, I communicated my thanks to his Bishop, in London.

Alex Lawson was a senior chief engineer with whom I was on most friendly terms, and we sailed together on a number of C.Y's ships. Alex was a small, fine-boned man with waved silver hair and classic good looks. A bottle of gin lasted a full week with Alex, as we indulged in only one aperitif at dinner time, he with gin and tonic, and I, with a pink 'un. He was a follower of his local team, Aberdeen F.C., and he spoke of little else, until one day, Alex was troubled by a heart attack. At least, that was my diagnosis. We were not equipped to help him, beyond the meagre contents of the ship's medicine chest, which only suggested remedies of 'last resort.' The ship was most of the way across the Atlantic, closing the West Indies and bound into the Gulf of Mexico. We were outside the range of any rescue helicopter. I re-shaped our course to make contact with the islands somewhere near to Puerto Rico, where I knew the U.S.Coast Guard kept such craft available. I was aware that it might well cost Alex his job, which caused me to 'drag my feet' a little. His engineers were anxious about him, but no more than I. I had to be sure the diagnosis was correct.

'You don't care enough about him,' they said, as no rescue plane came along, 'you only care about delaying the ship.'

The happy ending was that the 'copter did respond to my call for assistance, just as soon as he was within range. We made the rendezvous, and Alex. disappeared skyward, on the end of a winch wire. The diagnosis was of a troubled heart. He was hospitalised in San Juan, recovered and was flown home, but never went deep-sea again.

On board *Pacific Prominence,* Li was a Chinese chief steward thrown in with a Filipino crew and British officers. No one knew how he got there, it was one of the infelicities of our company's personnel placements. Sadly, Li did not possess any of the firm, no-nonsense bonhomie of a *maitre d',* nor did his manner of supplying the basics, come near to being defined as 'generous.' Li had his cabin on the officers' deck, one deck below mine. I received, one day, a deputation of officers.

– Filipino Monkee –

'That cabin was meant for an officer,' said Paul, our Chief Officer at the time, 'we don't want the likes of that fellow Li, in there. Please will you tell him to get below, on the next deck down, with the crew?'

On British ships the Chief Steward never had been an officer but, by a quirk of precedents, had often lived with them. It was a convenient arrangement. When you found yourself short of a bar of soap, you just went along and knocked at his door.

In this matter there was, though, a now familiar racism working its devilry.

I had a sudden flash of inspiration. The label above Li's cabin door, riveted there since the builder's yard, said CHIEF STEWARD, it was his rightful place, the original plans must have said so. I could not accede to their request. Li must stay where he was, I told him. Li, I believe was grateful. But a short time later he applied for a relief, and, to my surprise, got one.

Coal was the mainstay of our trade and thus our livelihood. We circled the globe for it, finding it in the unlikeliest of places, such as the old port at Sydney where we squeezed under the Harbour Bridge to find our berth in a tiny hidden corner.

But coal cargoes were becoming cheaper, less attractive. The crises in the supply of oil and its soaring price had thrown a scare into the world, lasting throughout the seventies. Some power-generating sources saw coal as a clear substitute, creating a demand, which in turn was answered by the expansion of open-cast mines in countries such as Colombia, and sprawling rail-head ship-terminals at Roberts Bank in Western Canada, Richards Bay in Natal, and Hay Point in Queensland.

To match this increased supply, the numbers of new ships, purpose built to carry it had multiplied, as new owners saw the rich profits to be made, alas too late. The oil crisis unaccountably faded, and the Middle East stitched up another uneasy peace. Oil prices became more affordable, while too many of the big empty ships chased fewer cargoes of coal. Where C.Y. Tung had led, many others followed. But C.Y. had 'got the cream' before the rates of freight now started to tumble. And C.Y. Tung was among the first to withdraw. We learned with alarm, that two of his carriers, less than nine years old, had been sold on the second hand market. The old redundancy fears trooped back again, making the ship a darker place.

They were still there, on a day when my *Pacific Pride* lay quietly alongside in the port of Ube, Japan, half-way through disencumbering herself of another coal delivery. The agent's runner from 'Nippon Express,' his yellow hardhat firmly held by its chinstrap, hurried aboard a little earlier than his usual eight o'clock, came no further than my dayroom doorway and bowed low from the waist. The telex that he handed me flew up off the page.

'On completion discharge, please proceed with all despatch to Shanghai, where your vessel is to be handed over to new owners.'

There were no 'regards' at the end, nor even a 'good luck'. It came from my Hong Kong bosses.

The impact ripped through the ship like wildfire when I released the news, as I knew I had to do. But the crew's unexpected delight in taking an early plane home, with a rich pay-off in their pockets, did not match my own feelings. With the ship went the job. Our small fleet made up a separate branch within the group. The tankers and the container ships had their own people, who jealously guarded their own. That anonymous telex seemed to spell doom for the palmy days of the bulk-carriers, with my job in the vanguard of it. Easy come, easy go, some said.

'It wasn't and it isn't,' I said.

There was no urgency. Not for me, anyhow. I took the long way out of the Inland Sea, in preference to the short crossing via Shimonoseki, not least because the charterer had offered me a bonus if I chose to take that exit without the expensive Japanese pilot. I knew the *Bungo Suido* well enough for that.

Which was more than I could say for the Yellow Sea and the approaches to Shanghai. I had never visited the People's Republic of China and the last time the Yangtze made my brand of news was when the British frigate *Amethyst* fought her way out of it in 1949, thus ruling out my visit there with cargo, long ago, aboard *Pacific Stronghold*.

Its flat featureless waters were marred by fishing stakes. They showed, in the dawn, as bobbing black staves taking root in the the sallow sea, as far as I could see, and I knew that earlier, I must have dragged a few of them under, unseen in the darkness. The estuary extended between horizons, without sight of land, though I knew it was there, from a sliver of incandescent light on the radar screen about five miles distant. I dared not go further and stopped the ship, to wait.

'Shanghai pilots, Shanghai pilots, this is the *Pacific Pride*, do you read me?'

We made the call, repeatedly, with no response. We waited, undismayed, willing to put off the moment. The very air seemed charged, different from ours. I was about to hand over my ship – to an un-seamanlike power, undeserving of it.

They all came at last, in a military looking boat. Two or three pilots, for the long sections of river and a number of officials, who bunched into my dayroom and clicked open their briefcases importantly.

'Captain, please, we have to ask of you one favour. We ask you to use your crew to drydock the ship. We have no crew of our own, yet.'

Strange people, I thought. How else would the ship get tied up, were we to leave her in mid-stream?

'By all means,' I said, politely.

– Filipino Monkee –

'Oh, and captain, we have found hotel accommodation for all the crew, whose flights have been booked to Hong Kong tomorrow. There were many, so we placed them, two in every room.'

I said, 'You will not put *me* in two to a room.' And to lighten the tone, I added, 'I want nothing less than the Penthouse suite!'

An older man, the buyer's Agent, remained serious, with a look of understanding in his eyes. To my surprise, he nodded wisely at my words. I was sure he remembered with regret the days before Chairman Mao, when many cargo ships came in with British masters who were men of substance. And, on the face of the same man was registered the purest apology, when a young fellow in grubby blue jeans with no hat and no baggage came up to relieve me, as the new captain of *Pacific Pride*.

I never suspected Shanghai of possessing such a Penthouse suite. It housed me on the topmost storey, in a ritzy apartment of three rooms furnished in the softest white leather and glistening chrome.

I joined the others in the morning for the flight out of Shanghai and back to Hong Kong.

Chapter Thirteen

A SORT OF ASSASSIN

My new-found friend, Captain John Ho, threw up his hands.
'Why did'n you give something to everybody ?' he said, in his accented English.
We were sitting side by side on the Kowloon ferry. John was about to introduce me to a new owner in search of a captain. My crew had already flown home. I had decided to stay for a while, making my presence well known, as this place was the most promising when seeking my kind of employment. Conversation had drifted onto the fate of my bond, my precious store of whisky, gin and cigarettes, which I had handed over to the Chinese before leaving Shanghai. It did not dwell anywhere near as much upon my last hours sleeplessly balancing the books, ensuring the integrity of that last honest dollar nor the pile of paperwork I had dumped, all properly complete, on the desks of the C.Y. Tung accountants.
'Your ship was sold,' John enunciated firmly, 'as is, where is, at the dock in Shanghai.' He looked me squarely in the face. 'There was nothing to stop you giving your bond away, before you got there.'
We threaded through the dense streets of Kowloon. John Ho, crisp and bouncy small, turned out in satinised suit, collar and tie, was brandishing his telescoped umbrella dangerously, while pointing out landmarks and we soon arrived at the office of the Seashine Navigation Company, whose business was the manning of other people's ships. There was a new vessel, the *Century Hope* owned by Mitsui of Japan, soon to

The Kowloon ferry.

need a captain. John Ho had recommended me. We chatted. I could go home, now. Give them my phone number, please, and they would call me. This was the kindest act by John Ho, it cancelled out all the irritations I had experienced as a result of his importunate radio messages.

My leave, welcome helpings of long awaited restoration, had hardly begun it seemed, before the people at Seashine kept their promised word. With my passage booked, I was to take the plane to Puerto Ordaz, far up the Orinoco River, in Venezuela, where I would find the ship.

A newer version, but similar in all basic designs, to my now familiar Hong Kong Panamax, the *Century Hope* was to load bulk ore for Dunkirk, in France. There was no difficulty in this. But chief among the telex messages piling up upon my new desk, with reminders of recent date, were warnings of grounding on soft mud at the Orinoco river mouth. A number of ships had stuck there, requiring powerful tugs, ordered from distant ports, to remove them, some with hull damage. I was to be guided by daily notices issued by the local river authority, advising the maximum sinkage permitted, thus limiting my lift of cargo. Their figures came in tenths of a metre and varied each day, based on surges of the river bottom mud. Also, I wondered, could they be tinged with a degree of optimism by an authority overly keen on its export figures?

– Sea Like A Mirror –

*Two identical sisters, **Century Hope** and **Century Progress**.*

Seashine's manning of *Century Hope* was different from the near-democratic set-up at Furness, and Tung. A tight control was placed upon Seashine by Mitsui, who, like British owners, saw the advantages of deserting their own Japanese flag. Its handling of men was not as sensitive, making, no doubt, its margins more profitable. Some very inexpensive officers came from Bangladesh, as did the crew.

The Captain from whom I took over, was Chinese. There remained, 'for company,' just two Englishmen, a Chief Engineer and a Radio Operator. They were unlike the average British seafarer.

The former of this pair was not long in looking me over. The Chief, a figure of considerable mass, came up on the first day, taking away all the light from my dayroom doorway.

'Say, I don't know if you're interested, but they do flights here for tourists, over the big waterfalls. We're heading up there this afternoon. Don't know if you care to join us?'

This suggestion was, at the least, impractical. I had the handover documents to prepare and a new method of accounting to familiarise myself with, before my relief flew out on the following day.

'Why could he not see this?' was my immediate thought.

I did not see him, or the 'Sparks', for two days. They came back, red-eyed, in the morning. The women, said the operator, with a leer, were 'great.' But his recollections, as indicated by his manner, had a sinister way with them that made me uneasy.

Three days completed our loading. We sailed out into the muddy river, for the day-long passage, drawing close to forty feet of water, our allowed maximum. The middle width of the river ran very deep and good speed was made down it. At the furthest outreach of the jungle scrub, where waterlogged clumps, widely spaced, emerged from the brown stream, the pilot took his leave. Here, the river emptied into the wide Boca Grande, and thence, the Caribbean Sea.

'You'd best put her on full speed, Captain. Maximum full ahead.' The pilot left me with a handshake, and these foreboding words.

The telegraph bells rang down, and with a gentle shudder, *Century Hope* started to make way. But within a minute or two, instead of the customary whispering as seawater made its brief contact with the hull, there came a deep quietness, with only the engines pulsing. She had, I knew, without looking over the side, 'taken the ground.' She was, put simply, stuck in the mud.

We tried the engines on maximum revolutions both ahead and astern, put the rudder each way to create a weaving motion, but she remained stuck.

I could visualise the headlines in next day's *Lloyds List of Shipping*.
'FIRST TRIP CAPTAIN GROUNDS ON WELL KNOWN MUD BANK'
We called back on the radio to the pilot boat, lying watching, a few miles back.

'*Keep going, Cap*, keep her going full. Keep on full speed – the very best you can do!' There sounded a note of panic, born of past experiences. We did, and more, phoning down for more revolutions.

'Emergency full ahead, please!'

And suddenly, with no sign other than a barely perceptible shiver, she started to move. Five minutes of pounding had, in some miraculous way, shifted the mud, though it easily could have had the opposite effect. We moved ahead. But then stuck again. And then again. After four hours of flying from elation to despair, and back, we slipped at last into unrestricted deeps.

While on passage to Dunkirk, our carpenter's hourly, then daily, function was to sound the bilges and wells, in case of bottom damage. Thankfully, we stayed dry. On arrival, I noted a protest with the French notary, a procedure by which, I understood, the matter could be respectably buried. The main casualty in the affair happened to be my full bush of a beard, now starting to show some white through the rusty black.

She was a lonely ship. I tried my French on the natives. I did not see much of my two compatriots, while in port. They were the first down the gangway, and the last up it. I had already remonstrated with the Chief about his lack of interest in the engine room, as he hardly ever went down. He resented any idea of an on board authority, and a spirit of rancour pervaded.

We sailed to the west again, for Norfolk, Virginia and a repeat of an Italian coal voyage I had made once before, with the cargo split between La Spezia and Venice.

Nearly there, only a day away from our first discharge port, I received a strange order from our Owners. It directed that I should not open hatches, until advised by them to do so. There was an overdue payment of the cargo freight money somewhere in the chain of merchant banks. Keeping my hatches battened down would retain the ship's possession of the cargo, until charges had been paid. The delay involved large amounts of capital and interest, matters which were not my concern. But I did know about the Bill of Lading, and that possession of it signified ownership of the cargo. This document had made slow progress, and was somewhere *enroute* between the U.S. and Italy.

My dayroom, upon arrival, was transformed into a busy accounting house floor by many excited Italian gentlemen.

'Please, Captain, I ask you to be reasonable, Sir!' said their spokesman. 'The documents are here, in *Italia*,' here his voice rose to a high note.

'We have sent a car, this morning, to Rome,' another continued, 'it will return this evening with the documents. Please captain, please give the order to open your hatches.' I felt all this was unnecessary, but for the moment, I was adamant.

One of the men I remembered from before. He acted for the electric company, the importers of our cargo, and liased with the discharging stevedores. We saw things in the same light. He returned on board, soon after the party had left, by himself.

'Really, you know, captain, the documents, truly, are in Rome. They'll be here before you have time to open up.'

The man seemed to speak the honest truth. Owners in Hong Kong were too far away, and not at all in the picture. I gave the order to open the hatches. Three days later, the charterers' broker called me to the phone, from his office in West Germany. He wished to repay me for my cooperation, he said, and did. My reward helped defray the cost of roof repairs to my house in England. With the lira, I purchased a money order in sterling that I mailed home that day.

Corruption? The thought was there. Was it the end product of some kind of malpractise, committed by me?

In business deals, like most seamen, I was without guile. The ways of modern commerce passed well clear of the ships and the men on them. Rarely had I been involved. Once, when as Chief Mate I had rejected rotten items in a cargo of 'new' potatoes, at Beirut, the shipper quickly came down and with a flourish produced his wallet, handing me a few crisp bills. This had, however, come after my company's agent had warned me that I should lie low, content with a muted entry in the Deck Log Book, in the cause of maintaining better 'relations.'

No new developments came out of my deals with 'big business.' I considered that my actions had been honest and above board. Nevertheless, I told myself, it had to be reckoned wth, and firmly resisted – the easy tumble from grace would not be difficult. Take care, my inner nature told me, and I had to listen, for there were few others to commune with.

'Take care,' it said, 'of that overweight Chief, who was never far away.'

Some of my conversations had been by radio, via the port control. It was difficult to keep him out of the radio room, where all communications had confidential status. The man was an avid eavesdropper and, I subsequently found, succeeded in twisting overheard fragments into scurrilous barbs.

Our ship picked up the pattern of trade again. Next came the bauxite from West Africa to Alcoa, in Texas. Then yellow corn from the Mississippi to Japan. And now towards Australia, for alumina, a refined bauxite for aluminium smelting, involving the long trip via Suez to Rotterdam and a port in Norway. This would complete another 'circumnavigation.' This navigation was now conducted by satellite whenever possible. But, in those early days there were few satellites orbiting, and the time lapse between position fixes was often prolonged. The satellite was, I conceded, a great boon when giving a wide berth to unmarked coral patches in mid-ocean, and the 'young Turks' among our navigating officers loved them, enabling them to discard most of the mathematics. I had, however, long decided that real navigation by hand-held sextant, by guess and by God and a good chronometer with dead reckoning, was a whole lot more satisfying.

Australia. We anchored in green water close by white sand, in tropical heat off the port of Gove, in the Gulf of Carpentaria, to await Immigration clearance. The Chief came up, demanding one of the ship's lifeboats for a visit to the town. I said 'no' of course. Firstly, the lifesaving equipment was not for leisure use, and secondly, we had not cleared the vessel inward.

At Gove, we replenished our fruit and vegetables, and a few dry stores. Small way-ports were expensive, but to have stored earlier, while in Japan, would have been even more costly. An unrelieved succession of remote and inaccessible places had put our food budget in the red. Supplies could be made to last through until Rotterdam, a matter of six weeks, as stocks were amply sufficient for this duration, and more. But some members of our crew were unhappy with the concept of restrictions. Items of food, such as tins of corned beef, were disappearing mysteriously from the dry storerooms which were kept locked at all times. The cook, a quiet Chinese whom I trusted, kept the keys. We were fortunate in having this man. He prepared economic meals of appetising quality. But he could not explain the nightly plunder.

The cook and the chief had, for some time, been at 'daggers drawn'. The big man regularly entered his galley uninvited, on the pretence of inspecting fan machinery, but nosed around instead, peering under saucepan lids and sniffing. About the middle of the Indian Ocean, things came to a head. The Chief was probing rudely with questions about his lunch, not long after consuming French toast cooked to order for his breakfast.

'What's this rubbish, then, cookie?' lifting a lid, followed by his mocking laugh.

Slow to anger, this was too much, and goaded the cook into a fury. He snatched up from his stainless steel bench the tool of his trade, a broad flat gleaming cleaver.

'Don' you mind what is that,' he cried, unsure and faltering in his English, and so brandishing his weapon ever more feverishly, 'you don't never mind, you …you … get out of here!' And he chased the Chief from the galley. The bully ran scared.

No stranger to violent attacks, the Chief took it well. He had told me, in cosier days, of how close he had come to the world of mayhem and murder. An active mysogynist, his attempt at a marriage had, unsurprisingly, failed, dissolving into bitter quarrels. He had been forbidden access to his children by a court, due to his threats, so he told me, and had now planned his ex-wife's demise in revenge. No one, in his right mind, would divulge this kind of information. I was not privileged to hear much more of it.

From Suez, I applied to Seashine for permission to have my wife accompany me while on the coast. She should join me in Rotterdam, crossing over on the North Sea ferry and go back home from Bergen, our last port in Norway.

It was a joy to see her. The bond between us grew stronger with time, and the long separation had starved my soul. I now had someone to talk to, civilly and with warmth, in English. I had fetched her in a taxi from the Hook. We made ready for sailing out of Rotterdam in the evening. The cook sent up a plate of sandwiches to the bridge. These were for the pilot, a not unusual provision on a long night's pilotage.

The phone on my dayroom desk gave a tinkle. It was the Chief. Lurking about, not far from his regular line of sight, he had spied out the steward, and the sandwiches borne up the companionway.

'I'd like to know something,' it was he who fired first, 'you two can have a pile of sandwiches on your supper tray, so why, may I ask, can't I?'

'The sandwiches were not for me, Chief. They are for the pilot.'

'The pilot doesn't normally get sandwiches.'

'Sorry. He does, this time.'

'I …'

'Sorry. I have to go up now.'

The man persisted, and I put down the phone. He continued to call, knowing that I had moved up to the bridge, and with the intention of embarrassing my wife. He chose the wrong girl. She also hung up on the nuisance.

Norway had a cleansing effect. We came to a wooden dock, bright with the freshest air, in the Hardanger fjord. Judy Gray and I walked each day to the village for coffee, returning on board to listen to my Mahler tapes. We took care to avoid any encounter with the Chief. After an idyllic stay of five foreshortened days, I saw her to the airport in Bergen.

Century Hope turned up on cue, in all the scheduled places, like a stage-set in a long-running show. Once again, she had arrived in the offing, at Panama.

The canal will not accept the loaded Panamax, without some trying tests. The ships were built to neatly fit the locks there, with only a few inches to spare on either side. The forces of compression must be overcome, especially in the triple locks at Gatun, by ship's engines run at full speed, merely to move ahead, inch by tedious inch. Also, there is little room under her keel, adding to the tight fit. The allowable sinkage in tropical fresh water (which was greater than cool water, and greater again, than salt) was an even-keel 38ft.6 inches and if this was exceeded, if she tipped or listed by just a couple of inches, canal transit was forbidden. You did not find out about it until initial entry was made, when unwelcome officialdom would stalk a ships' progress until able to read her draft figures from a place on shore. It was as well to get inside, and read the draft, as soon as possible.

Most vessels waited at anchor outside the harbour of Cristobal, in safe deep water, until invited to join the transiting line-up by the canal authorities. But the chief had been agitating again. The port of Cristobal, at the canal's Atlantic end, offered all the hedonistic delights closest to a sailor's heart. Only if she bypassed the outer anchorage and sought room inside the breakwater, could the crew hope for a night out 'in port.' She would need sufficient space to swing between the untidy lines of anchored ships. We really were too big. But the voice of the chief had the effect of water dripping on a stone, and, each day at coffee time, he had sidled up, politely 'bending my ear.'

'I suppose you know, Captain, if you could get a waiting space inside the harbour, there's a chance the lads might get a run ashore.'

'Alright, Chief, we'll see.' I said.

It would be a peace making gesture, at least, I thought, as we came up to it on a clear and rain-free afternoon and we can take a good look at the draft at the same time. I stood at the centre window of the wheelhouse looking for an open parking space while my heart stuck somewhere in the back of my throat. Could I squeeze her in? There was no turning back, there was insufficient room. The ship, somehow, managed to pick her way between the breakwater heads, moving through strange cross currents, enter the crowded inner harbour, find the last parking place, swing and safely drop a short nip of chain. The chief descended into a hired launch, and I did not see him before we dropped the pilot at the Balboa end. He was full of venom. The peace was not yet made.

We were all clear, and we had rung 'full away.' I had put my feet up, with a whisky at my side.

'Why so long, then?' he had appeared at my door. 'I'd have thought you'd let the boys up, sooner.'

'Normal stand-by, Chief. Rang full away soon as we could.'

'Bullshit!' He, a teetotaller, eyed my drink. 'What's up, you drunk, or somethin'?'

The bunker stop at Long Beach, was a regular feature of the voyage. Here, oil fuel was cheapest, and a deep draft presented no difficulty. We would top up all our empty tanks, enough for the Pacific crossing and more.

The broad expanse of open anchorage, with the preserved *Queen Mary* lying sedately at one end, spread itself in the morning sun. Our pilot boat flashed out from a gap in the breakwaters. We passed in, without a sound, to the bunkering area. Agents and officials flooded my cabin, bearing mail and empty forms for filling.

A wearying day. Even at first light, before arrival, we had 'calibrated' the ship's radio direction finding equipment. This was a statutory requirement, for long put off. Here in this port, due to a beacon which transmitted continuously, existed the ideal opportunity. While swinging the ship, we would compare its bearing, both visually and by radio. We had half finished this tiresome task, and would complete when we sailed.

It also happened to be the last day of the calendar month. It would be good to get the pay sheet balanced, have all hands sign it, pay them their money and mail it all off to Hong Kong.

The Chief also had work to do, there was no getting out of it this time. Taking fuel in an American harbour required his presence. A thimble full of oil spilled would call for his personal report and excuses.

Ships carrying fuel oil had seized the headlines for the past forty-eight hours in Long Beach and all the way up the coast as far as Alaska, for it was there that a loaded tanker, *Exxon Valdez* had just grounded. Large quantities of crude had leaked from her fractured tanks into the sea. The captain was, to a large extent, blamed for an error in navigation. Maritime agencies such as the U.S.Coast Guard were whipped up to fever pitch and lay in wait, ready to pounce on any offending merchantman.

– A Sort Of Assassin –

It was a long day. With our double bottom tanks full of fuel, hoses disconnected and bunkering barges away, we called for the pilot. The agent came for the mail. My accounts, all clewed up and sealed in a heavy envelope were handed to him.

'One hour from now, Cap, the usual thing, the pilot is ordered for then, Sir,' the agent, brisk and business like, stood up and made his departure.

'Let's put our feet up for a bit.' I addressed no one but the whisky bottle, who made an upstanding companion at the end of long working days. I poured myself a generous measure.

A pleasant evening. The anchor was quickly weighed, the pilot, a cheery soul, soon disembarked. There was the radio D.F. to finish calibrating. It would not take more than a few minutes. The breakwater beacon stood out like a sore thumb. I would approach it, swing the ship about a half mile off, with two officers taking bearings, tired though we all may be, it must not be put off this time. The main engines would be kept on standby until the exercise was complete. No one would be 'stood down.' And that included the Chief, who may never understand, and for sure, would not try.

''Bout time we got "Full Away", aint it?' That would be him now, on the engine room phone. 'What are you guys playing at, up there?'

'Tell him we have to finish calibrating, it won't be long,' I said.

'We're tired too,' I muttered regarding my two Bangladeshi officers, waiting motionless for my call, eyes glued to their bearing circles.

'Steady on,' I glanced back at the man on the wheel. He was fed up, too. We had swung all seventy five thousand tons of her through a full circle, lining up on the lighthouse at every compass point.

'People must wonder what on earth we're doing,' I tossed at the man, over my shoulder.

We were rudely interrupted. Chief had trespassed onto my bridge. He was standing next to me, not damp with sweat and oily waste in his grip, as I had reckoned on, but in his eternal, unbecoming grey shirt and shorts. The engine room phone had not seen hide nor hair of him this day. An angry Chief, who had, it seemed, been peering through his cabin window.

'What are you doing, for Christ's sake? The boys down below want "Full Away" and you've got her weaving all over the ocean. Are you trying to put us all ashore, or are you drunk?'

' I'll thank you to get off my bridge,' I said. The man had been told, in advance, of our calibration plans. He did not comprehend the procedure.

'You must be drunk,' he said. 'I warned you before about this.'

He could smell the whisky. I should not have had that second one, I knew that now.

'I have a job to do. Get off my bridge, if you please,' I repeated.

'Right ! You asked for it!'

Much more familiar with bridge workplaces than his own, he found his way to the phone in the radio room, without my knowledge. He selected Channel 6, and called the U.S.Coast Guard.

The Coast Guard's written report later recorded that the Chief Engineer of *Century Hope* called in to report the master drunk, with his ship 'weaving about all over the place.' Nothing could have had a more electrifying effect on the lurking Coast Guard. The furore resulting from the *Exxon Valdez* incident made headlines every day.

The Coast Guard boarded the ship, insisted we returned to port and anchor. I was not permitted to give my account. My blood test showed levels of alcohol 'just over the drive limit.' Other reports were called for. My outward pilot swore that I had behaved like a perfect gentleman. The agency manager ashore, an old friend, confirmed the orderliness of our visit.

But City Hall and the newspapers were not to be denied. To allow the situation to cool, it was suggested that I leave. I flew home from Long Beach the following day.

Chapter Fourteen

THE WORST SEA DAY

Retirement. This was a state in which you found yourself when too old to work. The latter condition, most surely, did not apply. Yet the prospect now hung dangling before our eyes. We would sell up and move to France, a country we both loved. Property was cheaper there, and we could live comfortably on the proceeds, until our pensions matured. We had some years ago, purchased a small Spanish *finca*. That could go into the 'melting pot' as well.

The status of the sea life that had sustained us, had changed so much. Flags and crews of the lesser maritime nations had swamped our own, and the traditions we had built on now seemed to count for nothing. It was not that there were no *other* traditions. Only that it was far too late to convert, and, in any case there were few of the old British companies remaining.

As one door closed ... it was time for another change. Our lives had seen a number of them and had been enriched thereby. My wife relished the challenge, as I did, and our long separations would be a matter of history.

We put the house on the market. That market was a fickle and mercurial one, a waiting game in which all of us played. But the Bank did not join in. The dwindling balance of day to day expenses would not wait.

'What are we going to do?' my wife said.

'I'll try the coast,' I said, 'that'll buy the groceries, *and* keep me closer to home.'

– Sea Like A Mirror –

Great Yarmouth feed importers. I skippered both of these before **Paloma**.

The coasting trade had always appealed. The 'dirty British coaster with a salt-caked smoke stack' of John Masefield's fancy had an unimpeachable, homely feel about it.

It only called for my name to be placed with various owners. The phone soon started to ring. I occupied a berth on two small ships, before I came to the *Paloma*.

The *Paloma*, of 643 gross tons, was registered, for convenience, in Puerto Cortes, flew the flag of Honduras and belonged to a Cornishman. She was cosily settled in the drydock at Rochester, on the Medway, when I joined. Her 1960s British design and build still showed thirty years on, through years of hard wear. The top deck was taken up with my suite of rooms, now turned seedy, which included a high sided maple wood bunk and a terrazzo floored bathroom.

'Found what you're looking for, chaps?' I addressed the backs of a group of shipyard men in boiler suits, who occupied my cabin. They were standing round a dog-eared plating plan which they had rolled out upon my cleaner desk, leaving me nowhere to put down my suitcases. Their leader looked up, troubled. They could not close the hatches, he said, as the mate had gone home and he was the only one who understood their fickle ways. North Sea storms, when dumping their ten ton waves

The Worst Sea Day

had distorted them and the years had rusted away their critical tolerances. The yard men went away, and set to with their acetylene gear. With flashes of bedazzling blue, they trimmed off a little here and added on a bit, there, and everywhere, making the best they could out of her decrepit carcass.

It did no good, but this did not show until that day in the 'Bay.'

The owner was in the machine shop. He came up at lunchtime with a box of pasties, from the pub close by. We all sat around, munching.

'What *I* should do,' he said, while we discussed the severe gales now being forecast, as we were sailing that day for Rotterdam, 'is sail down channel through the Downs, then turn her around, and steam up-channel with any westerlies right up your rear.'

It was the season of storms, and this one vaunted itself as no other I had ever seen. Leaving Rotterdam, the gales did not abate and progress towards our discharge berth at Teignmouth was impossible, leaving no alternative but to anchor in Margate Roads and await the briefest lull. On my weather facsimile, a chain of Atlantic depressions appeared as small, punchy and round as musket balls firing in from the western approaches. They would, on smelling the land, melt and curdle, conjoining as in my boyhood the globules of mercury on my science lab. bench linked up as if by magic, forming a more formidable whole. The developed isobars wove a mass of spidery lines from west to east, manifesting constant westerly gales piling the seas higher and higher, with no one to call a halt or limit them.

Our next loading was at Fowey, in Cornwall, a consignment of china clay for Seville. Again, we waited for a lull before putting the bow outside that cosseting harbour. But within a day, the skies blackened angrily and the Channel was again full of shrieking winds, spinning drifts of foam across a wild grey sea. Each wave was an approaching fortress wall up which the little *Paloma* hoisted herself, labouring with propellor racing and standing on her rounded rump, before tipping and slithering down the other side, half sideways. Our route turned the corner at Ushant. This was regarded as the entry point to the notorious 'Bay.' And now, the wind and sea came from the side, instead of ahead. The ship was more vulnerable on this heading, as seas could break over those flimsy hatch lids when she lay in the trough between the larger waves.

For two days she endured this punishment. I felt it, perhaps more than the others, as I was a 'big ship man.' Big ships did not go under so often. The sea state worsened, further. *Paloma* shuddered with each blow as huge lumps of green water struck then broke, surging across the ship, hiding the main deck from view. There was never any doubt – she would not survive this treatment, she was too small, too old and worn, might even break in two. We 'hove to'. There was no adjacent land for which we could run for shelter, so that this was the only option left. It involved a reduction of engine speed and alteration of course putting the wind nearly right ahead, so riding out the storm. While engaged thus, of course, we made no progress towards our destination.

My crew of four souls huddled in the messroom, doing what they could to hold down any moving articles while clutching onto something solid to preserve themselves. The outside world, at the other side of a radio call, had little time for us. Our owners in Plymouth, to whom I gave my report whenever I could, were powerless to help. Our only salvation lay on the deck in the small space outside the wheelhouse door. A small, round plastic valise, secured in place by a quick release slip, would inflate into a liferaft if thrown overboard into that churning sea. All we had to do was jump twenty feet or so into it, choosing the right moment, before it blew away.

The storms came winging in, successively. We all wondered, 'How much longer?'

There is a limit to staying 'hove to', exercised more by the heart than the head, as a constant fixed stare at the malevolent power of foul weather will convince an optimistic observer of changes which are not truly there. We looked for an improving shift of wind, a change in the set of the swell – hard to recognise as it takes place beneath a topping of creamy white crested waves. In any case, I pondered, we would have to make a run for it sometime, if we waited for that shift of wind to the north we might still be here in a month from now, without fuel.

At five in the morning of the third day, I switched the steering out of automatic and took the wheel myself. She seemed to be coping momentarily better. With firm handling, we could turn and run with the wind on the quarter, behind us, pushing us along. I feared she might end up in the trough, perhaps even unable to extricate herself, but knew that the risk must be taken. I waited for a lull, real or imagined, and put the wheel hard a port while increasing the engine speed. Her engines never failed her and to my great relief neither did the steering. She responded, and lurched around in spasms, dancing as gaily as an open rubber dinghy. The wind now from astern blew the funnel fumes into the wheelhouse, it gave an impression of speed. I planned to run in towards the Spanish coast, gambling that by the time we got there, conditions would have improved, and we could resume our proper course, our passage to Seville.

This was, in the total of my sea time, my worst sea day, one in which I was truly frightened. I was never so thankful as when I found, as we approached a dangerous lee shore in the form of the rocky coast towards Santander, that the wind had moderated and the sun warmly shone down. Our passage was resumed.

The mate went below to inspect the state of the holds and cargo. He, like the shipyard men back in Rochester, suspected the watertightness of the hatches.

Richard was a black haired Cornishman and, like most coastal men, blunt and very much to the point.

The Worst Sea Day

'Tons of water down there, Skip,' he advised, 'we'll get most of it out with the bilge pump, but not all of it.' But the worst part of it was that salt water had a corrosive effect on the china clay.

I communicated this fact, in my next phone call to the owner.

Having welcomed his ship back from her deals with the elements, not without some relief, it seemed, he responded to my report as I expected, having experienced similar mishaps in the past.

'Don't you go into Seville with that lot.' he snapped. 'Get shot of the wet stuff. We can't stand any more claims, and that's an order you won't get in writing, Skipper.'

We stopped the ship in the Bay of Cadiz, and hidden by the starry dark, the four of them 'got below' and shovelled overboard, in buckets, the wettest of the clay, before a great citrus-coloured sun came up over Cape Trafalgar.

If the time had not been close to Christmas, our broker would have worked us back up to the north, but Europe was closing for the holidays, and he found us a stop-gap cargo of loose metal scrap at Seville, for the island of Madeira.

A sun-blessed four day leg to Funchal should have made a welcome break, but for the coastal men the open expanses of ocean with no visible land at its edge provoked unease. They wished for visible land close by, and more. A visible supermarket. Food, or the lack of it, was by now making dinner time an occasion for dark looks and tetchiness. The company supplied no victualling. The crew purchased their own. There had been a long sad history of greed and misappropriation and this was the result. Unfortunately, the average crew member joined without a penny and relied on the storeroom leftovers of his predecessor. This may have worked for two-day trips upon the coasts of northern Europe, but did not here and now. And, after a long interval, there was little likelihood of their money going on food, on their first 'run ashore' in weeks. Each of the four took his stint as cook, but none was qualified and all were sadly improvident. We would just have to last until we got home, there were still some potatoes in the locker, and a slab of fatty mince.

Madeira was not easy to find. Our owner, always thrifty in his navigational purchases, had supplied no charts of the island regions. Once past the meridian of ten degrees west, I relied on an old school atlas, drawing my virtual map of the port from a full scale Atlantic chart. We anchored well out, following the same path as other ships.

From Funchal, our vision was of a speedy return home. But these wishes were quickly dashed. We were fixed for a cargo of pit-props arriving at the quayside in Foz, Portugal. We were to take them to Safi, in Morocco. This, again, did not please my crew. Although my contract paid a straight monthly wage, the crew emoluments were in direct relation to the cargo carried. They received a number of pence per ton for each cargo lifted. This method proved acceptable when the ship was in northern Europe, carrying a cargo every two or three days, even allowing time for breakdowns, repairs and awaiting fixtures. But now we had carried only two cargoes in fifteen days, earning them the barest pittance.

At Foz, the rigs loaded with pit-props rolled alongside in an unlimited flow, filling holds and on deck until the ship's stability was at risk and, with great difficulty, I stopped them. But there was not enough weight in tons to please our crew.

We took another load of scrap metal from Casablanca to La Corunna, where the good tidings finally came. At Bayonne, a cargo of wheat awaited us, bound for home, to the port of Wivenhoe.

'We'll make it for the New Year, then, Skip?' this from our sea lawyer. Every ship has one of these. Their questions are usually loaded, and have a quavering edge to them, emerging as a threat.

'If you get out and push, sailor,' I said.

But, I speculated, how would he suffer the latest developments? We were steaming across the deserted corner of the Bay, separating France from Spain. At the first hint of a distant ship's troubles, they had all come up, craning their necks, to listen.

The bridge radio, always tuned to the distress frequency, had crackled out the on-going drama, the spoken Mayday messages put out by the crew, the searches by sea and air, finding the oil slick, the awful spectacle of flotsam. Up to the north, a day's run from us, a coastal vessel of *Paloma*'s size had sailed from Rochefort, into a force ten gale. She had sunk, with all hands. They found the skipper in the sea, face down, somewhere off Noirmoutier.

'The poor buggers had grain,' one of them pronounced, making a fairly sound assumption.

'And left it lying loose,' another said, 'so it all shifted.'

'Them as had'nt got boards, should not be takin' the stuff,' said Richard, the mate.

And there, in the ways of all seamen, the matter rested, and was forgotten.

The law demands that measures are taken to prevent shifting grain, either by inserting fixed vertical shifting boards and loading each side of them or, alternatively, to stow on top of the loose grain a height of eight feet of the cargo in gunny sacks.

The *Paloma*'s shifting boards had been lost or stolen years ago. This dictated the second option, securing the grain surface with a height of bags, filled with the cargo. The standard written charter party stipulated that empty bags, already paid for, would be supplied. I made my request, by radio, after they had all gone down. The people ashore did not let me down. Awaiting us, on the dock in Bayonne, reposed five hundred empty gunny sacks.

– The Worst Sea Day –

'What! Bag up that lot?' the sea lawyer shouted, 'you ain't getting me to do that!'

'Now then Harry, its for your own good,' the mate said.

A withdrawal of labour was close at hand, our own little strike. There was no bagging. Later, there were signs of 'coming round.'

'They're not even offering something extra,' grumbled the sea lawyer, 'what's it worth, then, Skipper, they'll have to give us *something* for doing it.'

Not much to an owner. We sailed three days overdue, with an extra six pence per ton to be distributed, which was not over-generous, as the bags were extra large.

There is a constant flow of these little ships at Wivenhoe. They line the bank as far as Colchester, their brightly coloured hulls in ever changing postures of trim and inclination. When finished, they'll go down and anchor in the stream, looking for new employment, and hanging about like Mr.Micawber, quite sure that something will turn up.

But new employment was not for me, I had done my stint. The house had been sold for a goodly sum. We found a water mill in France, far, far removed from the sea, and left the phones to ring and ring.